The Healing Handbook

by
Norvel Hayes

HARRISON HOUSE
Tulsa, Oklahoma

Unless otherwise indicated,
all Scripture quotations are taken from
the *King James Version* of the Bible.

6th Printing
Over 40,000 in Print

The Healing Handbook
ISBN 0-89274-704-8
Copyright © 1982 by Norvel Hayes
P. O. Box 1379
Cleveland, Tennessee 37311
(Formerly *7 Ways Jesus Heals*, ISBN 0-89274-235-6)

Published by Harrison House, Inc.
P. O. Box 35035
Tulsa, Oklahoma 74153

Contents

Preface

Because the Lord has given me a healing ministry, He has dealt with me to teach about the different phases of healing.

There are many different ways to be healed, many different things for you to do. You need to learn in fine detail what to do. You need to get the Word on the inside of you.

You will get the Word inside you if you sit under teaching, but just going to church services won't heal you. The best church is not as good as the Gospel according to Matthew, Mark, Luke, and John. You must study the Bible. Look up chapter and verse for yourself. Quote the verse. Claim it. Say, "That's mine. I've got it!"

When you learn from God's Word what you're supposed to do and that your obligation is to obey it, the Word will work for you all the time.

Once you've got the Word on the inside, you'll start quoting it; and when you do, God will start performing it. God looks over His Word to perform it. (Jer. 1:12.) But unless you get the Word inside you, it's not going to come out of you.

Although some ways are easier than others for people to receive healing from God, healing will work for everybody who obeys God. If you're blind, God wants you to see. If you're crippled, God wants you to walk. He wants to give you whatever you need, but you have to claim it.

When you were born again by the Spirit of God, you became a citizen of heaven. You lost your citizenship on earth, though you still have the earthly identification of being an American, or a German, or an Englishman.

Heaven is a real place, just as America is. When you become a citizen of heaven, you gain the right to have anything heaven offers just as an American citizen has a right to anything America offers. As a citizen of heaven you have a right to healing. To receive your healing, all you have to do is claim your rights.

I have received hundreds and hundreds of testimonies from people who were operated on by the Holy Ghost after reading the first book I authored, *How To Triumph Over Sickness*. The Holy Ghost even operated on the editor of the book who had suffered from a particular disease for fifteen years. As you read *The Healing Handbook*, give the Holy Ghost your attention long enough to get it settled in your spirit once and for all that you can get your healing. If you do, I guarantee that you will be healed.

1

Jesus Heals
Through Your Faith

The best way to receive healing is through your own faith.

Your beliefs are based on the way you were taught. Was everything that you were taught true?

According to 1 Corinthians 12:2, *Ye know that ye were Gentiles, carried away unto these dumb idols, even as ye were led.*

The way you believe God today is the way somebody led you to believe Him. Think about where you are today. If you were taught according to the Scriptures, then you believe God according to the Scriptures.

If you listen to people who listen to God, who know Him and know something about the Bible, you will find it easy to believe the Bible. You will be led according to the Scriptures. If your belief is based on the Word, God can easily manifest Himself to you in the form of healing.

Base Your Beliefs on the Word

Many people in the church world today are ignorant of God's blessings because they've never been taught about them.

Some people think that only what their church practices is what's taught in the Gospel. They think that a church that believes in miracles, healing, and casting out devils is weird. The people in those churches aren't weird; they're scriptural!

The truth is that the ones who are weird are the people who don't believe in these things. If you don't want to be weird, then find out what the Lord Jesus said and start obeying Him.

Faith is the substance of things hoped for, the evidence of things not seen (Heb. 11:1). Your faith is your substance and God's Word is your substance. Your faith needs to be based on God's Word. *Without faith it is impossible to please him: for he that cometh to God must believe that he is, and that he is a rewarder of them that diligently seek him* (Heb. 11:6).

First, you must have faith in the Scriptures, in what the Bible actually says, in following God's instructions. There are scriptures for everything people need: for those who are lost and for those who need miracles and healing.

Second, you must diligently seek God by grabbing hold of your scriptures and, like a tiger that's crazy with hunger, refuse to turn loose. Faith as the substance means showing God that you'll do something right then.

I tell people all over the country that they can't afford to believe the Bible in any way they want.

God Wants To Heal You

The idea that God can heal you if He wants to is far from what the Bible teaches. Some churches teach this idea, but Jesus won't give sight to a blind person who says, "If the Lord wants to heal me, He will." God can't work through that kind of believing.

God would heal people in every church in America if the people knew that He could. But God won't heal if the people don't know that He will. God only performs according to what you know. The part of the Bible that you know as truth is what God will give you. If you haven't made up your mind that all the Bible is true or that God will give you what the Bible says He will, then He won't.

The deacons and heads of a church must believe that God's healing power is available. The Church is weak because weak men are in authority. The only part that weak men should have in a church is to warm the pews, help pay the bills, and sweep the floors.

God works only through the strength in the Church. Jesus, the Head of the Church, gave all the power He had to the Church. All power is in Jesus' name. The sooner you realize that, the sooner you'll use Jesus' name to combat the Devil. Jesus is not going to do anything else. We have His name and His power. All we have to do is obey Him. It's up to us to talk about God's healing power, to shout and sing about it, and praise God for it. That's what brings it into manifestation.

God's healing power will lift a cripple out of his wheelchair and make him normal. It will heal a deformed child right before your eyes. But the average church doesn't know or believe that.

Until people talk about it more, that kind of power will never come into manifestation in the average church in America. You must prove it to people by reading them the right scriptures. You must hold the Bible up to the congregation and say, "Healing power is available to you in this building. All you have to do is to learn how to get it!"

If you don't tell people that it's available, it will never come. A deformed person could go to the same church every Sunday for fifty years, but without knowing that God's healing power is available, he would never be healed.

If you say, "God will heal me if He wants to," you're letting in doubt. God wants to do everything the Bible says He'll do, and He'll do it for you if you'll believe it.

God's Test

God wants to heal you. No matter what might be wrong with you, God can hardly wait until you pass His test.

One time God explained to me what passing His test meant. He said, "The Bible is My test. My salvation verses in the Bible are a test for sinners. My healing verses are a test for sick people. My miracle-working verses are a test for people who need a miracle. Son, when people look to Me as their miracle worker, I create things for them."

The Lord Jesus is personal: He becomes to you exactly what *you* say He is. If you don't call Him *your* healer, then He won't be. If you don't call Him *your* miracle worker, then He won't be. He *is* a miracle worker, but not yours. He becomes to you exactly what you say He is. He will fulfill all your needs: make you rich, make you strong, make you clearminded, give you peace.

I never have sad or confusing days. When the Devil tries to put confusion on me, I won't accept it. Sometimes confusion *starts* to get hold of me; I may have a few seconds of confusion. But when it starts, I recognize it and say, "No, I won't be confused. I take authority over you, Satan. In Jesus' name, go from me." When I pray, Jesus gives me peace in my mind. No confusion can stay.

After ministering to myself, everything in the world seems to stand still before me. I can look at it with contentment.

God wants you to keep His peace. It's hard to believe the Bible when you lose His peace. It's hard to believe the Bible when you're without the patience of God. Faith is patience. God doesn't answer prayers that are prayed from nervous faith and He doesn't bless ignorance. If you're sick and remain ignorant of what God says about healing, He will let you die. The test to be passed is over chapter and verse.

When you get born again and become God's child, you have a right to the "goodies" in Matthew, Mark, Luke, John, Romans, Acts, and all the rest of the Bible. The Bible is your inheritance from God. God loves you individually. He loves your body individually. He can hardly wait to heal you. Not only will He heal you if you muster up enough faith, but He will delight in doing it.

I went to grade school with a boy named Jimmy Maynor who was a midget. When he was twelve years old, he just stopped growing. He was completely normal otherwise, as were his brothers and sisters. His parents spent thousands of dollars taking him to doctors all over the country for help, but nothing worked.

When he graduated from high school, Jimmy was four feet nine inches tall and weighed ninety-two pounds. Everybody called him "Pee Wee."

Because he was so little, he worked with the young people in the church. Even though the young people loved him, Jimmy didn't want to work with them. He wanted to be normal. He wanted to date girls like most teenaged boys do, but no girls would go out with him. Some of the boys would get him blind dates with girls who were five feet eight inches tall. To kiss them goodnight, Jimmy had to climb up on the car!

Today Jimmy is six feet one inch! He passed God's test! The only thing wrong with him is a little hump on his back.

When he was still a midget, he and another fellow were riding in a car that was hit head on by a drunk driver. The other boy was killed. The impact loosened Jimmy's leg bones and drove them through his hips until they were protruding out his back. The doctors in Cleveland, Tennessee, couldn't do anything for him, so they sent him to Chattanooga. The doctors there said he was like a bunch of hamburger meat. They just put him in a room to die.

Jimmy had been unconscious since the wreck, but in the middle of the night he woke up long enough to cry out to God. He begged God to let him live. He said, "Lord, I don't want to meet You like this. You've been trying to get me to work for you, but I wouldn't. I've never done anything for you. I've been rebellious. Jesus, if You'll heal me, I'll work for You as long as I live."

To the doctor's amazement, Jimmy woke up the next morning. After about a week, they started tying two-pound weights on Jimmy's feet to pull his bones back through his hips. In about a month, the bones were back in place.

Through the entire ordeal, Jimmy had been praying and reading the Bible; but then one day a spirit of fear came into him when he overheard a conversation between the doctor and a nurse.

Thinking Jimmy was asleep, the doctor said, "It's a shame about what's happened to this little fellow. I don't know whether he'll live or not; but if he does, he'll never walk again. There's no hope."

After Jimmy had been in the hospital for nine months, his family took him home in an ambulance. One day as he was reading the Bible, he discovered 2 Timothy 1:7 — that the spirit of fear comes from the Devil! *God hath not given us the spirit of fear; but of power, and of love, and of a sound mind.*

When he read that, Jimmy said, "Spirit of fear, I break your power over my life. I will walk again and be normal!"

Slowly, his body began to grow! Ten months and several pairs of trousers later, at the age of twenty-six, Jimmy was six feet one inch tall!

He then began to share his testimony in Southern Baptist churches. When he told about what God had done for him, he drew large crowds. The people were astounded when they heard his testimony.

One night a few years ago, Jimmy asked me to go to a meeting with him. When we got together, he said, "Norvel, I've had constant pain ever since that car wreck years ago."

He was surprised to hear my answer: "Jimmy, you don't have to put up with pain; I don't. You need to get baptized in the Holy Ghost and receive power from on high to take authority over pain. Don't take anything from the Devil."

He got excited about what I had said and, soon after, asked God to baptize him in the Holy Ghost. At noon one day, he sat down and read the Bible to seek God for the baptism. The Spirit of God came upon him and baptized him in the Holy Ghost. Jimmy learned how to take authority over pain. When he found out what God had for him, he passed God's test and used his own faith to receive his total healing.

Wrong Beliefs Can Kill You

Denominational churches don't know very much about God's healing power. The Southern Baptists are not ashamed of salvation. They boldly practice John 3:16. Baptist ministers can preach some of the best sermons in the world, but the things you learn from their salvation sermons won't help when the Devil visits you with some physical affliction.

The people in the Southern Baptist church where I was raised didn't know anything about having healing services. The members of my church used to say, "God can heal if He wants to. God can do anything." That's a cop-out! As long as you're ashamed of the Gospel, God will never heal you. If you are ignorant of what the Word says about healing, the Devil can come in and claim your life. When people took diseases in my church, they died. There was no such thing as a blind person receiving sight or even a bad cold getting healed.

My mother and father were honest, down-to-earth, old-fashioned Southern Baptists from Tennessee. They never did their neighbors any harm. I never met a man who was better than my dad. Daddy was always the same. He wouldn't have told a lie for a million dollars. He was a man who couldn't be bought.

I remember one time he told a man that he'd sell him a piece of property for a certain amount of money. While the man had gone to get the money, another man offered Daddy much more than what the first man was giving him. Daddy said, "I can't make a deal with you. I've already given the other man my word. If he has the money, he can have the piece of property. If he doesn't have the money when he comes back from the bank, I'll sell the property to you."

The second man wanted me to try to get Daddy to take his offer for the property. When I told Daddy about this, he said, "Son, I can't do that. I've already given my word to the other man."

You know what I told him? "That's what makes me enjoy calling you 'Daddy.' "

He just grinned.

My mother and father were good Christians, but being good Christians has nothing to do with believing the Bible. My mother died at 37 of cancer and my brother died at 19 of Bright's disease. Healing was for them, but they didn't know it. They had nobody to instruct them.

The Devil Causes Disease

After I was baptized in the Holy Ghost, I began to pray to find out why my mother had died when I was 10 years old. My sister was 11½ then, and my brother was 14. When the mother of three little children dies with cancer, it's horrible. The children don't want her to die: They cry and wring their hands. They only have one mother. People come in all the time and tell them, "Jesus loves you. He knows what He's doing."

If you say that to little children about their mother's death, they'll think, "If Jesus loves me, why did He take my mother?"

Some people's belief about love is so warped that they identify death with love. When the Devil kills someone in your family, Christians ignorant of what the Word teaches tell you that Jesus loves you and that He knows what He is doing. It's true that Jesus knows what He is doing and what He was doing had nothing to do with the death. The average Christian will try to connect something that the Devil did with Jesus. In John 10:10 God states plainly that

19

the Devil is here for three reasons: . . . *to steal, and to kill, and to destroy.* Jesus today is just like He is in the New Testament and He never killed anybody in the New Testament.

After I had prayed for three days to find out why my mother hadn't received her healing, the Lord began to talk to me.

You may say, "I wish God would talk to me that way." If you pray long enough, He will. If I had prayed for only two days to find out the answer, I still wouldn't know why my mother died; but after I had prayed long enough, the Lord answered me.

Very plainly, He said, "I didn't kill your mother. Neither did I have anything to do with her death."

I said, "If You didn't have anything to do with my mother's death, why did You let her die? She didn't want to die. She loved You; she was a Christian."

Jesus told me that my mother wasn't healed because of *where* she went to church. He said, "Listen closely: Your mother couldn't receive My divine healing power because her church didn't teach the people how to receive their healing. People only receive what they are taught how to receive."

In other words, Jesus was saying, "I came that you might have life and have it more abundantly. [John 10:10.] I've come that you might be healed. Don't blame Me for the Devil's work."

None of the bad things that have happened to your relatives were God's timing or will. As long as you keep your mind cluttered with lies, you never will learn the truth. If you have your mind made up that God's will involves sickness and death, you can't learn the truth.

God's Fire Purifies

You have to rid your mind of lies. Kenneth Hagin tells about the day he shut himself up in the sanctuary to ask the Lord what was wrong with his church. Even though the church had many members who were giving more money than ever before and more souls were being won than before, something was wrong.

After Brother Hagin had prayed for hours, the Lord came and told him that he needed to make a certain decision. He said, "Look on the inside of you."

When Brother Hagin did, he saw a dark spot. He said, "Lord, what's that?"

"That's some of your church doctrine that has fastened itself upon your spirit."

Brother Hagin had been baptized in the Holy Spirit years before and had been praying in the spirit and praying for the sick since then. He said to Jesus, "I thought I got rid of that years ago."

"You didn't rid yourself of all of it, and it's been robbing you for years."

Watch yourself to make sure you believe the Bible exactly as it's written. Believe God that you're going to get victory. Even though you're saved, baptized in the Holy Spirit, and love God from the top of your head to the bottom of your feet, you may still have let men's ideas and doctrines inside you. Get rid of them.

Let the fire of God burn the old doctrines out of you. John the Baptist said to get baptized with the Holy Ghost and with *fire*. (Matt. 3:11.) Most Pentecostals and Full Gospel Christians, who have been baptized in the Holy Ghost and speak in other tongues, have never been baptized with God's fire.

When the Lord touched me, He wanted me to follow Him and believe the Bible, but I couldn't. I asked God to touch my mind so that I could. For three years I prayed for mercy.

After I was baptized in the Holy Ghost, I got on the floor and prayed in tongues so long and so hard that groans replaced the tongues. The Holy Ghost brought the fire of God upon me and burned out all that church doctrine. When I got up, I felt as though I'd been drained totally. I felt clear and clean from the top of my head to the bottom of my feet. Then it was easy for me to believe God for anything.

To believe God, you have to pray and read the Bible. You have to work at it. You have to pray yourself into heaven, into the holy presence of God.

If you'll allow yourself to be baptized with the fire of God, it can burn those doctrines out of you making it easy for you to believe the Bible. When you believe God *can* do anything, He *will*. Your spirit will be so free that you can easily walk up to a cripple or to a deformed or blind person and say, "God wants to heal you."

Make Up Your Mind To Be Healed

God loves you. His healing power is a gift. All you have to do is receive it as a gift.

As I was getting ready to speak at a convention of the Full Gospel Business Men's Fellowship in Canada, God's presence filled my room. I had planned to give my testimony about being baptized in the Holy Spirit, then give an invitation for people to receive the Holy Ghost; but I found out that the Lord wanted to teach something before that.

Jesus spoke these words to me: "After you are introduced today, I want you to teach first what blind Bartimaeus did to get Me to heal him."

I gained a new respect for healing and faith when the Lord told me that. Often a person will search out new churches to see what God will do for him, to see *if* God will heal him. Jesus wanted me to emphasize what *blind Bartimaeus did* to get his healing. He was healed on *his faith.*

And they came to Jericho: and as he went out of Jericho with his disciples and a great number of people, blind Bartimaeus, the son of Timaeus, sat by the highway side begging.

And when he heard that it was Jesus of Nazareth, he began to cry out, and say, Jesus, thou son of David, have mercy on me.

23

*And many charged him that he should hold
his peace: but he cried the more a great deal,
Thou son of David, have mercy on me.*

Mark 10:46-48

To find out exactly how blind Bartimaeus was
healed, we need to look at what he did. When you
study the Bible, you need to find out what it actually
says, not what you think it says after only lightly
reading over it.

Jesus gave me a specific order: to teach what
blind Bartimaeus did. Bartimaeus did two things: he
asked and he thanked God for it.

Ask

The first thing that blind Bartimaeus did was
cry out. That's the opposite of wondering whether
God is going to do it for you, as many people do. The
scripture says he began to *cry out and say* . . . .
Notice that the first word that came out Bartimaeus'
mouth was *Jesus*.

Look at the ministry of the disciples who walked
with Jesus. The Bible says, *Many charged him that he
should hold his peace* (Mark 10:48). The people who
walked with Jesus didn't believe very hard.

Blind Bartimaeus couldn't afford to listen to
them. If he had, he would never have received his
sight. The people who go to your church may have all

kinds of ideas about what the Bible says. You can't base your beliefs on them. You have to believe the Bible 100 percent!

If people believe only 90 percent of the Bible, the remaining 10 percent will rob them.

The second thing blind Bartimaeus said after calling out for Jesus was *have mercy on me!* Jesus loves to hear things like that. Words like those get His attention because He is so full of love and compassion. I have never known Jesus not to respond to any human being as long as that person had even a little bit of faith, even if he was lying in a gutter somewhere. It doesn't matter whether he's black or white, the biggest sinner in town or the best Christian in town. I have never heard of somebody crying out for mercy and Jesus turning His back on him. Jesus will *always* respond!

When the people tried to get blind Bartimaeus to be quiet, he cried even louder. This reveals why 99 percent of Christians don't receive their healing: either they don't cry out or they cry out only a few times.

I've had to learn some of these things the hard way. If you don't watch yourself, the Devil could attack you with some affliction that's hard for you to get rid of.

Sometimes I'll take a thirteen-member team with me and train a church in how to take the salvation message door-to-door. Once when I was in a church in Mississippi raising up one of these teams, the Devil hit me with weakness and a fever so bad that I had hot perspiration running off my nose. I prayed, but the more I prayed, the worse I got. By the third day I was so sick I could hardly walk. I decided that I couldn't go outside, that I had to rest. As the day went by, I got even worse. By late afternoon I hadn't even taken a shower yet. I was sitting there so sick that I wanted to die and go on to heaven.

The Devil said to me, "You have to get someone else to speak tonight because you can't make it to church. You feel so bad; you can't even get dressed."

The Devil is nuts, and sometimes he gets himself in trouble by talking too much. From the natural standpoint my body was too sick to go, but when I heard him telling me that, I got mad at him for trying to bombard my mind. I jumped up and screamed, "Satan, you're a liar!" Then I yelled, "I'm going to church tonight!" I ran to the bathroom, jerking off my clothes as I went, jumped in the shower, and let the water hit me right in the face.

I said, "Satan, I'm taking a shower to get ready to go to church because Jesus is my healer. My body is healed, in Jesus' name!"

I kept repeating those words, and the split second that I got out of the shower, all the symptoms disappeared. I felt God's power go through me from the top of my head to the bottom of my feet. I was totally healed. I came out of the shower room feeling like a sixteen-year-old.

26

Be like blind Bartimaeus: Don't have any quitting sense and don't waver. If you feel so bad that you can hardly stand it, just lie on the floor in your own living room and cry out to God for mercy and for healing. Cry out (for hours if necessary) that Jesus is your healer and that God's healing power is for you. Keep on and on. Sometimes when I've felt so bad that I couldn't do anything, I would cry out for over thirty minutes and God's power would come through me and totally heal me.

I guarantee that when you cry out as blind Bartimaeus did with no quitting sense, you'll get heaven's attention. The 49th verse says that because blind Bartimaeus got Jesus' attention Jesus *stood still*. We see in the same verse that Jesus *commanded him to be called*.

> *And they call the blind man, saying unto him, Be of good comfort, rise; he calleth thee.*
>
> *And he, casting away his garment, rose, and came to Jesus.*
>
> *And Jesus answered and said unto him, What wilt thou that I should do unto thee? The blind man said unto him, Lord, that I might receive my sight.*
>
> *And Jesus said unto him, Go thy way; thy faith hath made thee whole. And immediately he received his sight, and followed Jesus in the way* (vv. 49-52).

Jesus said to blind Bartimaeus, *What wilt thou that I should do unto thee?*

27

You may say, "Jesus knew what was wrong with him. Why did he have to ask for his healing?"

James 4:2 says, *Ye have not, because ye ask not.* God wants you to ask.

If you want healing, ask Jesus for it. Raise up your voice and ask Jesus to heal you. Go to him like a little child of God and say, "Jesus, I need a healing."

After you've asked, confess Jesus as your healer. God's healing power will come to you. Jesus said to blind Bartimaeus, *Go thy way; thy faith hath made thee whole.* The blind man immediately received his sight.

Blind Bartimaeus' cries to God were his faith. God hears the cries of a blind man. He hears the cries of a lonely heart. When the cries get His attention, He heals.

Once when I was speaking in Canada, God told me that if one of the people in the congregation — a man in a wheelchair — would cry out like blind Bartimaeus had, he would be healed. After I worked with the man for a while, he began to confess. After he had cried out for about five minutes, God's power suddenly fell on him. He sat in that wheelchair for a few more minutes weeping, still crying out. Then he got out of the wheelchair and walked across the church.

The pastor said, "He has never done that before!"

I said, "He's never confessed like that before!"

He wasn't embarrassed to cry out, and he got healed.

Don't Be Ashamed

You must boldly talk your faith, no matter where you are. As I was walking up the steps of an office building one day, I was hit with a pain in my right knee. My knees suddenly gave way, and I had to hobble to get to the top of the steps.

When I got to the top, I raised my knee, pointed at it, and said, "No, you don't!" People were going up and down those steps. I'm sure it seemed strange to see a fellow standing at the top of the steps, pointing toward his knee and screaming at it; but I wasn't concerned about what they thought. You have to be willing to confess the Gospel as soon as you need it and not be ashamed.

I said, "No, you don't, Devil! You can't make my knee give way on me. I won't accept this!"

After I had sat there for a while and confessed the Word, my knee got normal. On level ground I could walk just fine, but the next time I started up the steps, my knee did the same thing.

I said, "No, you don't. God's power is in my knee. I call my knee normal, in Jesus' name!"

This happened every time I walked up the steps for the next six months. The longer this went on, the louder I got. I had to boldly obey the Scriptures, even if talking to my knee did look strange. One day I walked up the steps and at the top suddenly realized that my knee hadn't given way. It was totally healed and has never given way since.

You have to make up your mind that God wants to heal you and that God honors faith. You have to show the Devil that you're going to have what is rightfully yours and not be embarrassed.

I have been set free from all binding spirits that made me ashamed of the Gospel. I'm not ashamed of any part of the Gospel. I'll cast the Devil out of a person while we're standing on the steps of the First Baptist Church if I have to! People look at me as if I'm strange, but I don't care. You have to let the Holy Ghost change you so that you don't care what people think; then you can be free and as wild as I am!

Sometimes you have to forget about being nice and polite. When I see a person dying with a disease, I don't want to be nice to the Devil! When you get tired of the Devil always trying to fasten cancer or some other disease on you or your family, you will be ready to stand up and take authority over the situation. You will be willing to talk your faith loudly. The stronger and louder you talk your faith, the quicker God works. If you just walk around quietly saying, "Jesus is my healer," Jesus will heal you, but it might take Him four or five years.

When I was healed of the flu, only about five minutes had passed from the time I had jumped up from the couch until I had gotten out of the shower.

Don't care what you look like to other people; just be wild. Most people won't even be wild at home in front of their families. You have to be careful that your pride doesn't allow the Devil to take advantage and beat you into the ground. Sometimes you have to confess ruthlessly. Don't let embarassment over crying out to God keep you from being healed. You ought to be hungry to obey. It doesn't embarrass me to walk around for an hour in front of a congregation, telling them to say to Jesus, "Have mercy on me." It shouldn't embarrass you to go forward at a meeting and cry out to God to get your healing.

Only Jesus can heal you. No matter what price you have to pay, you must cry out until you get Jesus' attention. The biggest price you will pay is hurt pride. Exactly how long it will take you to pay that price and exactly how many cries it will take for you to get healed, no one can say. The main thing to remember is that you have to pass God's test.

When I walked that day into the ballroom at the Full Gospel Business Men's Convention in Canada, I had no idea why God wanted me to teach what blind Bartimaeus had done first to receive his healing, but I knew enough to obey God.

The ballroom was packed with people. I walked up the steps to the platform and sat down in the one chair that was left at the head table. I knew only two or three people on the platform. The fellows sitting on either side of me were strangers. The service had already started so I scooted in without introducing myself.

In a few minutes the master of ceremonies stood and said, "We're going to change the order of the service. Before I introduce our banquet speaker, Brother Norvel Hayes from Tennessee, we are going to hear a testimony from the donut king of Canada about what the Lord means to him."

The man owned a donut empire, which sold hundreds of thousands of donuts a day. He was a multi-millionaire.

One of the fellows sitting next to me, a very distinguished-looking man, pushed back his chair and started moving toward the platform, feeling his way. I watched for a moment before I realized that he was blind! Then I understood why the Holy Ghost had told me to teach first on what blind Bartimaeus did to get Jesus to heal him.

After the man had testified and returned to his seat, the master of ceremonies introduced me. I explained what had happened to me that afternoon, then said, "I'm going to teach you exactly what blind Bartimaeus did to get God to give him his sight." I wanted that blind man to thoroughly understand what I was talking about. As I was teaching, I would lean over from time to time in his direction and say, "Blind Bartimaeus kept on crying out. He kept on and on and on."

The people in the congregation were sitting on the edges of their seats, waiting for the donut king to cry out so that he could get healed. They wanted him to cry out, but he was a man with a great deal of pride. Having millions of dollars won't cause God to do something special for you. Whether you're a pauper or a rich man, you have to obey the Scriptures in the same way if you want to receive from God.

The blind man never cried out. He had to be led out after the meeting because he was still blind. He didn't receive because he didn't cry out. He was two verses of Scripture — and maybe two or three hundred cries — away from healing. The Lord Jesus Himself would have restored that man's sight if he had obeyed God.

God has a great deal of mercy and He wanted to share some of it with that man. He told me specifically what to teach that day because He loved that man and wanted to heal him. God had the power to give him his eyesight; but even though he was a born-again Christian who loved God, he needed to claim his healing in order to receive it.

Wounded pride is a small price to pay for receiving your healing!

Give God Thanks

After you've cried out to put your faith to work, as blind Bartimaeus did, then receive your healing by faith, in Jesus' name. Look up to heaven and thank

Jesus for healing you. The Bible says, *In every thing give thanks* (1 Thess. 5:18).

First: Ask God.

Second: Thank Him for it.

Open your mouth and say, "Father, I'm asking You for my healing, and now I want to thank You for doing it. I believe in Jesus' name that it's done."

Close your eyes and tell Jesus that you love Him. Yield yourself to Him. He'll give you your healing as a free gift. You may see something that you've never seen before. He'll perform operations for you Himself.

You overcome by the blood of the Lamb and by the word of your testimony. (Rev. 12:11.) When Jesus heals you, tell somebody. Say, "I accepted my healing today, in Jesus' name." If people don't want to hear it; tell them anyway; it will build your faith.

Before Jesus fed the multitude as described in Matthew, chapter 14, He let His voice go to heaven and said, "I thank You, My Father, for feeding these people and for bringing Your blessings to them."

God heard His voice. When Jesus thanked God, power was released. God performed a miracle and multiplied the five loaves and two fishes to feed more than 5,000 people.

You may say, "But that was Jesus doing that!" Yes, and you have the same clean Spirit living in your belly that Jesus had in Him. That same Spirit goes through your body and wipes out disease. When the disease leaves, you feel very clean. That Spirit is what makes you feel so clean.

Don't forget to give thanks after you've received your healing, when you are strong and healthy.

Every morning, first of all, thank God because your name is written in heaven. (Luke 10:20.) Then say, "Thank You, Lord, for Your healing power." I say this every day, even though I'm not sick. I thank the Lord that His healing power is working in my body to keep it strong and that my body is functioning normally.

The number one way to receive your healing is to follow the instructions in God's Word. However, if you can't get your healing in this way, there are other scriptural ways to receive.

2

Jesus Heals Through
The Laying On of Hands

We see in the following verses from Mark's Gospel that Jesus laid hands on people:

> There came a leper to him, beseeching him, and kneeling down to him, and saying unto him, If thou wilt, thou canst make me clean.

> And Jesus, moved with compassion, put forth his hand, and touched him, and saith unto him, I will; be thou clean.

> Mark 1:40,41

Notice how the leper approached Jesus for his healing. Humbling himself, he knelt down before Jesus and respectfully expressed his faith. When the leper, broken out all over with that incurable disease, knelt down before the Lord and said, "Jesus, You can make me clean," Jesus was moved with compassion.

Jesus is the same yesterday, and to day, and for ever (Heb. 13:8). He has never changed; His

37

compassion has never changed. If you approach Jesus in the same way that leper did, He will heal you, too!

When I was holding a meeting in Atlanta, Georgia, the Lord said to me one night, "When a sick person comes sweetly to the altar as the leper did, kneels down before Me, and says, 'I've come to receive my healing, Jesus,' My heart goes out to him. My love and compassion flows."

Jesus put forth His hand, touched the leper, and said, *I will; be thou clean;* and the leprosy departed. Laying hands on people is a doctrine of the Church.

In the following passage Jesus is telling the believers to continue His ministry:

And he said unto them, Go ye into all the world, and preach the gospel to every creature.

He that believeth and is baptized shall be saved; but he that believeth not shall be damned.

And these signs shall follow them that believe; In my name shall they cast out devils; they shall speak with new tongues;

They shall take up serpents; and if they drink any deadly thing, it shall not hurt them; they shall lay hands on the sick, and they shall recover.

So then after the Lord had spoken unto them, he was received up into heaven, and sat on the right hand of God.

And they went forth, and preached every where, the Lord working with them, and confirming the word with signs following.

Mark 16:15-20

Much of the ministry in the New Testament is through the laying on of hands, one of the doctrines of the Church.

In verse 16, what is *he that believeth* believing? Jesus is talking about the Gospel in this verse. The whole New Testament is the Gospel: salvation, healing, miracles, laying on of hands, and special miracles through handkerchiefs and aprons.

Verse 15 states the Great Commission: *Go ye into all the world, and preach the gospel to every creature.* From verse 18 we see that part of the Gospel is the laying on of hands. Going into the world and preaching the Gospel to every creature means preaching about the laying on of hands. If you go to church where the ministers don't lay hands on the people, that church isn't obeying the Gospel. Obedience to the Gospel includes the laying on of hands. When you preach about this doctrine; then do it — lay your hands on a sick person; God's power will heal him.

Jesus Commissioned All The Church

The laying on of hands is for *all* believers and *all* churches. The casting out of devils is for *all* believers and *all* churches. You just have to learn how to do it. Ministers call me and say, "Brother Norvel, the Lord wants me to go on the road with you. I'll pay my own way." They stay with me from two to four weeks and just watch me cast out devils and pray for sick people.

After watching the way Jesus gently works to heal people for several weeks, they take what they've learned and go back to their own churches. When they start obeying the Scriptures themselves, God changes their whole church.

Learn To Lay Hands on the Sick

One time when I was speaking at a banquet in Georgia, God proved to six pastors, who had never had healing ministries, that God heals people through the laying on of hands.

The banquet room where we met was packed. While I was speaking that night, the Lord moved on me to say to the congregation, "If Jesus has never healed anybody physically through your hands or healed in any other way through your ministry, come and stand before me. The Lord wants me to say a prayer for you."

Six ministers came up. I asked what denominations they were from, then said, "All of you are pastors of Bible-believing churches. Do you believe in the triune Godhead?"

They said, "Yes."

"Do you believe that Jesus died on the cross for you, that He rose from the dead, that He is sitting on

40

the right hand of the Father, making intercession for the Church, and that the Bible is true?"

"Yes."

I told the ministers to stand around me; then I put my hands on theirs and said, "Father, these men are Your chosen vessels, called to preach the Gospel and to bring people into heaven. I ask You to put the same anointing of God's healing power that You've put in my hands into theirs. I ask You, in Jesus' name, to anoint them with Your healing power, to let it flow from my hands into theirs right now, and I thank You for doing it. I claim it to be so, in Jesus' name."

I was acting on directions straight from heaven.

I said, "We are going to see miracles and healing power come in here." I lined all the sick people across the front and divided the line into six sections. Then I told each of the six ministers to lay hands on the people in one of the sections. I said, "Instead of praying a long prayer, just tenderly lay your hands on the people and say, 'In Jesus' name, receive your healing.' Watch what God does; then go on to the next one."

The ministers did what I told them to do. Suddenly the healing power of God came on someone and caused him to drop to the floor. The pastor looked astonished, then looked down at his hands.

Those six pastors prayed for everybody in that big ballroom. By the time they were through the first healing line, they were weeping. They would look at their hands and say, "I can't believe this is happening to me."

After everyone had been prayed for, I said to the pastors, "Don't be ashamed to have healing lines in your own churches. Educate your whole congregation in one service. On Sunday morning tell your people this: 'Jesus loves you. He wants to save you and all your relatives; and He wants to heal you. Jesus is your healer.' Read them Mark 16, then say, 'God gives me an order here. He tells me to lay my hands on sick people. Because God loves you, He wants to heal you.'

"Call your people up and say, 'I'm going to do what Jesus Christ tells me to do. I'm going to lay hands on you, then tell you to receive your healing, in Jesus' name.' If you go down the line gently and quietly, the Lord will heal people and the congregation won't be offended."

To get God to work for you, you must obey Him.

Learn To Cast Out Devils

As we saw, Mark 16:17 says, *And these signs shall follow them that believe; In my name shall they cast out devils; they shall speak with new tongues.*

People say you ought to love first. You definitely need to know the love of God, but you also need to know your duties as a Christian. The first two things in the Gospel you should do is throw out the enemy and talk in a language that drives him nuts.

You can be a good Christian without casting out devils. Many Christians don't, even though Jesus tells us to do it. But if you don't cast out devils and speak in new tongues, you should start. The Church needs to learn first how to fight the enemy — how to cast out devils, in Jesus' name.

Sometimes I'll go to a church and ask, "How many people here cast out devils?" Hands will go up all over the audience. Other times when I ask that question, people will just look at each other instead of raising their hands. Even if they do cast out devils, they don't want to admit it.

If no hands go up, I say, "Jesus wants me to ask you another question: When are you going to start?"

That doesn't go over too well, but I didn't want it to. I deliberately make that kind of church nervous. Everything gets real quiet.

The Gospel was written by God to jar people's thinking. Unless you think scripturally, God doesn't want you to think like you do. You can have a church without casting out devils or speaking with new tongues, but it will be a weak one. You have to take authority over the enemy. You have to pray in tongues, or the devils will know what you're going to do before you do it. Don't be ashamed when you cast out devils and pray in tongues.

One time as I was speaking at the Sunday morning service of an Assembly of God church, the Lord showed me that there was a homosexual in the congregation. The church was overflowing with people. About two hundred visitors were there. I was going to be nice and wait until after the service, then take the young fellow over to the side of the room and cast the devil out of him.

I finished speaking, then prayed with the people who came up after I had given the altar call. The Spirit of God was moving so sweetly and blessing the people when the Lord said to me, "I want My ministry out in the open. Side-room ministries don't please Me as much as altar ministries. I want you to cast the devil out of that boy so that the church can watch."

I went over to the fellow who was about sixteen years old and had him stand up. I whispered in his ear, "You're a homosexual. I won't let the congregation know that, but I'm going to cast that spirit out of you right now. You want to be free, don't you?"

"Yes."

I said, "You foul spirit, in Jesus' name, I take authority over you and command you to let this young man go! I break your power now, so you have to obey me and come out of him. In Jesus' name, you can't have this young man. He belongs to God because I say he does. God made his body and you can't have it. Satan, his body belongs to God, and I command you to obey me. You foul spirit that's trying to wreck this man, I take authority over you. Turn him loose now!" I stood there calmly, saying this over and over. I must have repeated it ten times.

All of a sudden that thing broke loose in him and came out. God's power began to shake him so hard that I couldn't hold onto him. Then it knocked him flat on his back. He lay there quivering, crying, rejoicing, and thanking the Lord. Later he said, "I wanted so much to be free!"

The people in that church loved God. After they saw such a demonstration of the Holy Ghost, they couldn't keep from rejoicing. Nobody there knew that young man had been delivered from homsexuality; it was none of their business. But the congregation could see that he was free from something because of the way he was rejoicing.

Jesus loved that young man, and He wanted him to be set free from homosexuality. To be free, you need to have patience and not be ashamed of the Gospel, even if it means being delivered on Sunday morning in front of the whole church and two hundred visitors! Because I obeyed the Gospel and cast out devils, that boy was delivered.

To help a demon-possessed person, you have to do certain things. Take, for instance, people in mental institutions. If you are asked to go to a mental institution to pray for someone, do it only if God gives you instructions. You won't accomplish anything if the Lord doesn't tell you to go.

First, you have to bind up the Devil, in Jesus' name. Jesus said in Matthew 12:29 that you are to bind the strong man; that means the Devil.

Second, pray in the Spirit for God's will to be done for that person. Praying in the Holy Ghost will cause God's will to be performed. There are some things we just aren't smart enough to figure out and pray about in English. We aren't smart enough to know the different things that need to be prayed for concerning some people; but the Holy Ghost is! That's why we need to pray in the Spirit.

Third, when the person finds enough freedom, get him to start confessing that he is free.

Doing these three things will bring anybody out of a mental institution.

God Confirms With Signs Following

You must learn what God's Word says, then do it. When you do God's Word, you become established and your faith becomes stronger. Then you will know your rights in Christ Jesus and know that the Lord Jesus will do anything for you when you only believe His Word. God will confirm His Word with signs following. After you obey God by laying hands on the sick, God will heal them. If you cast out devils in Jesus' name, the devils will leave.

Tell The Truth

Sometimes if a pastor takes me out to eat after church, our conversation will go something like this:

"Brother Norvel, I wish I were like you. I want to say some of the things that you say, but I'm afraid to. I don't want to make my people mad."

I always answer, "Don't be afraid; just spit it out. If your people get mad, they'll get over it."

If you haven't been in the presence of God often enough for Him to share much with you, then you won't have much to minister to people. But once God shares things with you, you have to tell people what God has told you, even though you don't want to. The people will never get ministered to if you don't tell them.

Sometimes a person won't believe the Word at first, but later he will remember and believe it, even if he heard it six months before. When God says to do or say something, don't try to figure out why; just do it.

You should tell the truth. The church should be a place where you learn things about life and find out what God has for you, not a place where everything is kept secret. Churches should hold sex classes for young people and teach them exactly what to expect when they get married. So many young people are in the dark when they get married that afterwards they say, "I didn't know it was going to be like this."

Sometimes you have to blast people with the Scriptures in order for them to believe it. Some people at my meetings sit half-stunned when I tell them that the Spirit of God will heal them and put their homes back together.

They say, "I'm not believing my ears." But when I blast them with the Word, God does it!

When I gave an invitation one night, God told me to pray individually for the people standing in line. He said, "Take authority over the Devil. Then agree with each person in My name for his need. As two of you agree, My power will begin to work for that person."

I took each person by the hand and asked, "What do you want from the Lord?" Then I ministered in the way God had told me.

One of the people that came forward was a pretty brunette about twenty-eight years old. She said, "Brother Norvel, Jesus told me that if I would come up here and tell you about my problem, you could tell me what to do. I've never told anybody about this before: I don't want my husband to touch me. I don't let him. I can't stand for him to."

"How long have you been married?"

"About three years."

"Did you have sex with him on your honeymoon?"

"Yes."

"Wasn't it sweet?"

"Yes, it was. But after we came back, something kind of took me over and I couldn't stand for him to touch me. I don't know what to do. I can't tell anybody in church about it."

I hate the Devil! It would take the Devil to have a warped mind like that. God wants a husband and wife to be one, but the Devil wants them to be two.

I took her hand and said, "Devil, I break your power over this girl. I command you to take your hands off her marriage, her husband, and her body. I command you to set her free so that she can be a normal wife. She has the God-given right to be loved by her husband and to enjoy life to the fullest. She has a right to join with her husband and be one flesh with him forever. You're not going to steal from her! In Jesus' name, set her free!"

Then I told her what to do. I said, "You are free. Do you believe it?"

"Yes."

"Then you have to put action to your faith. When your husband tries to touch you, I want you to make yourself respond. You may not want to, but do it anyway. Make up your mind that you can do it, then do it!"

Jesus blessed me for ministering to that girl and her husband. I have seen them several times since, and God has done a work in their lives. He has given them three children.

Almost every time I go to that city, I see that precious family sitting in the congregation. One time I was able to visit with them in their home. When I first walked into the house, her husband said, "Brother Norvel, let's all hold hands and pray. The Lord used you to save our marriage, and we want you to ask Him to continue His blessing. For the first three years of our marriage, our house was cold and dead; but because you told us the truth, it has turned into a warm, sweet, beautiful home that is full of love."

As we stood there holding hands, the Spirit of the Lord swept in and swallowed us up. We just broke into weeping and rejoicing.

Don't be afraid to tell the truth!

God wants His tender love to flow in every room of a Christian home, and you can experience that love in your own family. Married couples must not allow the Devil to rob them of their pure sweet love and the precious moments they share as husband and wife. Don't let it happen. Claim your rights in Christ and refuse to let the Devil rob you.

Straighten Out Your Thinking

God is waiting for you to get your thinking straightened out so that He can bless you. It makes no difference how smart you are; it's what you do with the Gospel that counts.

A Spirit-filled teacher invited me to speak at Southern Illinois University where 22,000 students attended at the time. The university had made a rule to allow complete freedom of speech and press. To let the students hear a wide variety of views, the university was going to begin turning over the classrooms at night to different organizations.

In one classroom someone was going to teach about witchcraft; in another some people were going to present a homosexual play.

When this Spirit-filled teacher heard about it, he rose up and said, "Do you care if we have a meeting about Jesus in one classroom?"

He got permission to use a classroom and invited me to speak. The teacher said, "Brother Norvel, would you be willing to come and teach the Bible right next door to where they are having a homosexual play?"

I said, "Praise God, why not?"

I taught there for a week and a big crowd came.

One night I asked the people, "How many of you have seen Jesus heal people?"

Hands went up everywhere.

"I'm going to pray for the sick tomorrow night. You can come and watch God heal people all over this place."

The next night I prayed for the sick by the laying on of hands. I had the people come up on the stage. Even though it was ten times as big as a regular stage, there wasn't enough room for everybody.

After attending that meeting, one of the patients of the school psychiatrist told him to go hear me talk about God. He said, "This Norvel Hayes doesn't talk like a normal man: He talks wild! But I've been listening to him and my mind has cleared up, Doctor! I've been coming to you for years and have paid you a lot of money. In just two or three days, I've gotten help! This Brother Hayes takes authority over devils. You need to come hear him!"

The psychiatrist said, "He takes authority over devils? If this Norvel Hayes is as wild as they say he is, I might as well go hear him."

I had one morning class and one evening class each day. The psychiatrist came to a morning class. After the service, the people I was staying with told me that the psychiatrist from the university had called and wanted me to call him back.

When I did, he said, "Mr. Hayes, I've never heard a human being talk like you do. I don't know anything about what you were saying, but somehow it made sense. I need to talk to you. Would this afternoon be convenient for you?"

After we met, the first thing he said to me was, "My mind is telling me that all these things I've heard you say aren't true."

I said, "I understand that; but, Doctor, I'll help you now. Pull all the education out of your brain and lay it on the table. Believe the Bible, trust God, and listen like a little child. Let me reason with you. If I talk to you for an hour, I will still have two hours before service time. Ask me any questions you want. If I can't answer them, we'll look them up in the Bible; God has the answer in the Bible."

He agreed.

I said, "Doctor, I know why you can't believe what you've heard me talk about. Because you're a psychiatrist, you tell people how to live. But you haven't learned how yourself. You leave your office, go to the country club, and have cocktails with friends for an hour or two; then you go home. You've been doing this for years. Now that you're about 45 years old, you find yourself wondering. You look at the bottom of that cocktail glass and think, 'I spend all day teaching people how to live, but I don't know how myself. Is a cocktail glass and a country club all that life has to offer?' "

He said, "How do you know that? I've thought that many times . . . especially during the last few years. As I've sat listening to dirty jokes, I've wondered that very thing: Is this all God has to offer: a cocktail party after work at the country club?"

I said, "Sure, you've thought about that. Everything in the world gets old after a while because it has nothing to offer. It's all phony. But Jesus and the Holy Spirit don't get old, they are for real! I've already been where you are, Doctor. The Lord will make a new human being out of you and set you totally free."

After we had talked for about an hour, I asked, "Are you going to come tonight, Doctor? This is the last night."

He said, "I wouldn't miss it."

That night I gave the congregation a double dose. I spoke on healing — how to receive the power of God to get your body straightened out — then, on the baptism of the Holy Ghost. I gave an invitation for healing first.

I said, "If you want to be healed, come stand right in front of me so the Lord Jesus can heal you. He's the healer; I'm not."

The psychiatrist was the first person to get up. Because Satan had caused physical problems in his body, he didn't just casually get up — he jumped out of his seat! After he went up, some other people came and stood.

I said, "All you people that need more power from God, get out of your seat and stand on the other side of the church from the people that have come up for healing. Let Jesus give you more power."

The psychiatrist, in a loud voice, said, "Mr. Hayes, is it all right if I leave this line and get in the other one?"

The whole classroom laughed.

I said, "Take it easy, Doctor. You're too anxious."

He said, "I want more power!"

I said, "Take one thing at a time! Let the Lord heal you first; then get in the other line to receive power."

I prayed for the people in the first line and laid hands on them.

After I finished praying for the psychiatrist, I said, "The Bible says you are healed, Doctor."

He said, "I am?"

I said, "Yes, you are. Now that you are, go get in the other line so that you can get more power."

About fifteen minutes after I had prayed for him again, he was talking in tongues!

After listening to me and watching me for only two services, he began ministering to people. He told them that Jesus would heal them and give them power; then he invited them to his house. The people started getting healed and baptized in the Holy Ghost.

After I left town, the doctor called to tell me what was happening. He said, "The prayer meetings are getting so large that I can hardly get all the people in my house! I cast out devils just like you did. I say, 'In Jesus' name, come out!' I lay my hands on people and claim their healing in Jesus' name, like you did. God heals them all over the house."

If you've got any sense, learning how to minister to people's needs doesn't take very long.

The next year, the university called me back and asked me to stay for two weeks. During that year the psychiatrist had led his family to God. After my meeting, he had gone home and told his wife, who was an alcoholic, that God had healed him and baptized him in the Holy Ghost.

When she saw how well he was, she said, "If you can get something from God, I surely can."

God saved her and baptized her in the Holy Ghost; then He saved the daughter. That family was turned on to God! All of them took part in the prayer meetings and cast out devils.

According to the psychiatrist, his beautiful daughter had gone from being "way out in left field" the year before to being probably the strongest Christian in town. When God manifests Himself like that, it will get you straightened out.

When I asked the psychiatrist why his daughter's faith was so strong, he said, "She saw what God did for her daddy and mother. When I prayed for sick people, she saw Jesus heal them. She believes God can do anything.

"One time when she and her husband were walking in the country, a child fell in a well. The wall of the well was too high for them to reach down and grab the child's hand, and they couldn't find anything big enough to step up on to reach the child. Then they cried, 'God, help us!' Suddenly they saw a big rock by the well that hadn't been there before. God had created that rock in response to their prayer! By stepping on that rock, they were able to rescue the child."

When I was asked back to speak at the university a year later, I met the psychiatrist's family. His wife had invited me to their house for a meal. I could see that his wife and daughter were totally dedicated to God. Talking doubt couldn't shake his daughter. (If God made a rock for you, wouldn't you believe that He could do anything?)

Remember, the psychiatrist was a highly educated man. When he learned to obey the Gospel, God healed and abundantly blessed him.

Once educated people see the truth in something, they will believe it. I've won more doctors to the Lord than any other profession. God gives me favor with them. When I pray for doctors, God usually heals them. Then they put healing scriptures all over their office walls. God also gives me favor with chiropractors.

When I was speaking at a Full Gospel Business Men's convention in Memphis, I met a chiropractor and his wife who were members of a denominational church. They had never before been to anything like that convention. I was scheduled to hold a three-day meeting at a church in Kentucky when the Memphis convention was over, and it happened that they lived only forty miles from there. They came to me and asked if they could drive me there.

I had already made arrangements for the pastor of that church to pick me up in Memphis, but when they asked me to ride with them, the Spirit of God said, "Go with them."

On the last day of the convention, the pastor called my hotel room to find out what time I wanted to leave. I told him what the Lord had said for me to do and that I would be at his church in time for the seven o'clock service on Sunday night.

When the chiropractor and his wife drove me to church, I said, "Why don't you come in and stay for the service?"

The chiropractor said, "Do you think it would be all right? We've never been to this kind of church before."

"Yes, it will be fine. You can go as my guests. I'll get seats for you on the front pew."

That night I taught on healing, then I said, "If you believe Jesus is your healer and you want Him to heal you, come up here."

As soon as I said that, the chiropractor jumped out of his seat on the front pew and ran up to me. I laid hands on him and said, "Thank You, Jesus, for healing him." Immediately he was knocked back by the power of God. He fell flat on the floor. When his wife saw that, she came up and the same thing happened to her. The Holy Ghost healed both of them right there.

After that, he became a member of a Full Gospel church and is now an elder. Recently I saw the two of them on television. He said, "We didn't know Jesus healed today until we went to a church service with Norvel Hayes. He taught on healing and prayed for us. Jesus healed both my wife and me of diseases we'd had for years!"

3

Jesus Heals Through The Head of The House

As we saw before, Hebrews 11:1 says, *Faith is the substance of things hoped for, the evidence of things not seen.* Your faith is your *own* substance and your *children's* substance. Your children aren't capable of believing very much unless you've taught them the Word from the time they were little.

God Removes Growths

My daughter Zona wasn't healed at a church or in a healing service. She was healed at home. Her faith had nothing to do with her healing. She was healed through my faith and my confession. I confessed a verse of Scripture for forty days before her healing manifested. She told me my confession was driving her nuts.

Zona's body was covered with boils, knots, and ugly warts. They started appearing when she was eleven or twelve years old. I took her to a doctor and had them removed through surgery, but the knots came back and brought their cousins with them! By the time she was fifteen or sixteen years old, she had forty-two growths on her body.

By that time I had been baptized in the Holy Spirit and was trying to pray and believe God for her healing; but the more I believed God, the bigger the knots seemed to get! Zona's healing didn't manifest because I was ignorant. After I had prayed for three years, the Devil began to bombard my mind with worry.

When Zona started dating, it was embarrassing for her. She didn't have trouble getting dates, but she would say to me, "Daddy, it's embarrassing for me to date. I hate it when boys want to hold my hand. My hands are so ugly!" She wanted her hands healed so much that she called the doctor herself about having the knots removed again.

I was trying to study faith and learn how to confess it, but something wouldn't let me. I kept backing away from it.

About that time Kenneth Hagin and his wife came to stay four or five days with me on their way back from New York. When they got to my house, I was at my office, so they went to my neighbor's home and called me. As soon as they called me, I went over. The last time the Hagins had been in town for a meeting, these neighbors had fixed dinner for us.

All of us were sitting in the den talking when Zona and their daughter came in from school. Zona hadn't seen the Hagins for several months.

Brother Hagin said, "Zona, how are you doing, honey?"

"I'm doing just fine, Brother Hagin, except that I'm having trouble with my dad. He won't do what I want him to." (Teenaged girls always have trouble with their dads.)

Brother Hagin said, "What do you mean?"

"Look at my legs and my knees. See how ugly they are? They've got knots all over them. The doctors said that if I would come to the hospital for one night, he would put me to sleep and take off all the growths at one time; then I'd be free of them. But Daddy won't let me! I've been asking him for a year, but he keeps saying that he'll think about it. Will you talk to him?"

Brother Hagin said, "Zona, I can curse those things and they'll disappear."

When he said that, everything got real quiet. I looked over at the lady of the house and saw how displeased she was. What was I supposed to do? Brother Hagin would be leaving in a few days, but I had to live there next to those people! To change the subject I said, "The weather in Tennessee is really nice this time of year."

I had worked with Brother Hagin and knew him well enough to know that he was telling the truth, but I didn't know what he meant when he said, "I can curse those things." I knew how to pray for the sick, but I didn't know what he was talking about. He said it in the same way he would have said, "I can go to the store with a dollar and buy a loaf of bread. He said *he* could.

I had always thought that Jesus was supposed to do everything. Zona was a good Christian and loved the Lord, and I knew that Jesus loved her; but I had been raised in a church which taught that if you loved God, He would do something for you — if He wanted to. I thought God would heal Zona only if He wanted to.

I intended to ask Brother Hagin what he had meant when he said that he could curse the growths; but when we got home, we started talking and I never thought about it again. Later I wondered how I could have forgotten something like that. I forgot because God blocked my mind, and I realized later why He did: He wanted to tell me the answer Himself.

Around midnight Brother and Sister Hagin went to the guest room and I went to my room. A while later, somebody knocked on my bedroom door. I opened it to see Brother Hagin standing there.

He said, "Norvel, we had planned to stay with you for four or five days, but a few minutes ago the Lord spoke to me and said, 'I want you to get up early in the morning and go to Dallas, Texas. Your sister is going to die soon. When you get there, I don't want you to pray for her because I'm not going to heal her.

I healed her five years ago when you prayed for her and laid hands on her. I gave her five years of walking in divine health to build her faith, but she didn't study the Bible like she should have. Because she hasn't taken the time to build her faith, she can't believe Me for herself. The same disease that she was healed of five years ago has come back on her. I'm not going to heal her this time through your faith. This time, at the age of 55, she is going to die. She'll come to heaven because she's a Christian, but she's going to die. So get up early in the morning and go see her.' "

Refusing to believe God's Word, refusing to believe what Jesus said, can cost you your life. In Matthew 21:22 He said, *All things, whatsoever ye shall ask in prayer, believing, ye shall receive.*

The Hagins left early the next morning. About three days later, I got a telegram from Brother Hagin saying that his sister had died. He had been exactly right. If he hadn't left that morning, he wouldn't have seen his sister before she died.

About two weeks later, I was walking through the house on a Sunday night after the evening service. Zona was sitting in the den with her boyfriend. I had no earthly idea that anything unusual was about to happen to me. I was just walking through the living room thinking about how Brother Hagin could curse growths.

All of a sudden my natural senses were suspended. I was caught up into another world and

God began to talk to me. (I had seen the Lord once, but in this particular manifestation, I just heard His voice.) When God talks to you, it's not the same as when human beings talk to you.

The Lord said, "How long are you going to put up with those growths on your daughter's body?"

God will put up with your disease as long as you will. When I had the flu, He put up with it for three days because that's how long I did. When I got tired of putting up with it. I jerked my clothes off and jumped in the shower. Even though I had cold chills running all over me and occasional hot flashes, I boldly stood there with water hitting me right in the face and screamed that I was healed.

Because I was ignorant of my rights in Christ Jesus and because I was scared, when God asked me how long I was going to put up with those growths, I answered, "They're not on me, Lord! I don't have them, Jesus!"

When I said that, I found out how shocked the moneychangers must have been when Jesus ran them out of the temple. (Matt. 21:12.) God didn't waste any time telling me, "You're the head of your house!"

Then He said, "You belong to me just as Kenneth Hagin does. You don't need Kenneth Hagin to pray for your daughter. You can curse those growths in My Name just like I cursed the fig tree. If you believe and not doubt, they will die and disappear."

The passage of Scripture the Lord used with me was Matthew 21:21,22. In it, Jesus is talking to his disciples. He says:

> *Verily I say unto you, If ye have faith, and doubt not, ye shall not only do this which is done to the fig tree, but also if ye shall say unto this mountain, Be thou removed, and be thou cast into the sea; it shall be done.*
>
> *And all things, whatsoever ye shall ask in prayer, believing, ye shall receive.*

Notice verse 21 says, *If ye have faith . . . .* You must have faith and doubt not.

God is not the head of the house; the man is. God told me to curse the growths because I was the head of my house. When He told me that, I saw something most fathers have never seen: The things that go wrong in a man's house are his fault.

If a child has been sick for two years, it's not the child's fault and it's not Brother Hagin's fault; it's the father's fault. When he is weak scripturally and spiritually, he doesn't know his rights in Christ Jesus.

Because your name is on the deed, no devil or any kind of foul spirit has the right to operate or even to come on your property because you're the head of your house. No demon has any right to attack your wife and children. You have to know that because if you don't know your rights, those devils will walk right into your living room and try to put a disease on some member of your family.

I shouldn't have let the Devil put those growths on my daughter's body in the first place; and once they were there, I didn't know what to do. God doesn't bless ignorance, but He will always bless His Word. You can depend on that forever!

As soon as the Lord finished talking to me, my normal senses began to return. Soon I was standing again in my own living room. This wasn't something I dreamed up; it took me about five minutes to get back into the natural again. God restored my natural senses by degrees.

The very moment I had completely returned to the natural realm, the Devil said, "Don't go to see your daughter now. Her boyfriend is with her and you'll embarrass her. Have mercy. Wait until tomorrow."

Whenever you hear *Wait!* it's always the Devil. He will do and say everything he can to keep you from doing what God wants.

Jesus told me the same thing that Brother Hagin had told Zona: Curse the growths and they will disappear. I made up my mind then to walk into the den where she and her boyfriend were sitting and do what I knew to do. When I made that decision, then the power of God began to work in me.

The gift of faith began to rise up in me. All of us want to be nice to everyone. I wanted to be nice and not embarrass Zona. But power began to come up inside me, and I couldn't see anything except victory. I had power in my fingers, in my feet, and in my mouth.

I walked into the den and said, "Zona, I'm not taking you to the hospital tomorrow or any other time. I just got back from heaven. I talked with Jesus and He told me that if I would curse those knots on your body in His name, and believe Him for it, that they would die and disappear."

Then I put my hands on Zona and said, "You devil, I'm the head of this house and this girl belongs to me. These knots and warts have to get off her body, in Jesus' name. I curse them at the root and command them to die. Growths, in Jesus' name, get off my daughter's body! Thank You, Lord, for removing them."

When I finished, I turned and walked off, still thanking Jesus. Before I left the room, I said to Zona and her boyfriend, "Remain as you were."

As I walked down the hallway, I said, "Thank You, Jesus, for removing those dumb knots off my daughter's body. It's so wonderful to have a daughter with a body that's clear of those ugly knots and warts. She's free from them! Thank You, Lord, for removing them!"

I was talking my own faith in my own house!

I can't go to your house and claim healing for your family; I'm not the head of your house. God does in *your* home what *you* allow Him to do. If you haven't been doing much, He hasn't been doing much. The more you confess the Word, the more He will manifest.

The next day I went to the office saying, "Thank You, Lord, for removing all the knots and warts from my daughter's body. Thank You for doing it, in Jesus' name."

I must have made that confession of faith thousands of times for a month. I said it as I lay in bed, as I walked through the house, as I got out of the car, as I went to lunch.

One day I met Zona in the hallway. As a habit by then, I said, "Thank You, Lord, for removing all the knots and warts from my daughter's body, in Jesus' name."

Zona said, "Daddy, you've said that thousands of times for two weeks. I can hear you saying it when I get up in the morning and when I go to bed at night. You say it over and over, all day long. Look at me; the knots are still there! See?"

"No, I don't see anything except new hands."

"Daddy, you're driving me nuts! You can see them, can't you?"

"No!"

"Daddy, they are there!"

"Where? I'm looking through the eyes of faith. I'm calling you free from all knots and warts. They can't operate in my house. I'm the head of this house, and I say they can't!"

After about thirty days of confessing this over and over again, I was on the back porch one afternoon when Zona came home from school. She came to the door and said, "Daddy, I want to ask you a question. For two or three years there have been forty-two growths on my body. I count them every day. Today there were only thirty-four. Where did eight of them go?"

"I don't know, honey, but the only choice the other thirty-four have is to go with them! I'm the head of this house; and I'm not giving them any other choice."

Then I began to thank God for what He was doing: "Thank You, Lord, that my daughter's body is free from all knots and warts!"

Often I would sing as I walked back to my bedroom, "Thank You, Lord, for removing the warts and knots from my daughter's body." In the next room I could hear Zona answer me: "Daddy, they're not going."

Sometimes I would walk the floor and say, "Lord, it's so wonderful to have a daughter with a body that has no knots or warts. Glory to God! They've been cursed in Jesus' name, and they can't stay on her body. Knots, I'm talking to you. Warts, are you listening to me? You have to get off my daughter's body."

I could hear Zona saying, "My daddy is flipping out." Zona is bold in her speech: She says whatever comes to her. She gave me a hard time, but I acted as though she hadn't said anything and kept on confessing.

About a week later, I was standing in the kitchen, not thinking about anything special, when suddenly I heard a loud crash from Zona's room. She came running out of her room and down the hallway like a wild girl.

About halfway down the hall she started yelling, "Daddy, look at me! I've got new hands and new legs! I was hanging my dresses in the closet, and my hands were as horrible-looking as they've been for three years. But when I reached down to pick up another dress, I had new hands!"

She was holding her hands up, looking at them. God had removed every blemish! The skin on her legs, knees, hands, and arms was shining. It was rosy-looking, like a baby's skin.

She said, "Daddy, I know you love the Lord; I love Jesus, too. But my faith wasn't as great as yours. I've spent lots of nights in my room, weeping and begging Jesus to give me new skin. I wanted new hands more than anything else in the world. I can understand God doing something for you because you work for Him. But just think: Jesus loves high school girls like me enough to give them new hands!"

I took her hands and looked at them. When I did, the glory of the Lord rolled in. We stood there together, weeping.

Whenever I talk to Zona, she says, "When you tell about my healing, be sure to say that after the doctor removed the growths, they came back along with their cousins; but when Jesus removed them, they never came back!" Zona went from having the ugliest hands in her school to having the prettiest!

Throw the Devil Off Your Property

If the Devil gets in your house, use the doctrine of the Church: the laying on of hands.

If you say, "Lord, little Tommy was sick last month and now Betty's sick. We're a Christian family; I don't know why this had to happen to us. The Devil just won't leave us alone," you're as crazy and ignorant as the Devil!

You should shut your mouth, boldly lay your hands on your children, and say, "No, you don't, you dumb devils! In Jesus' name, get off my children's bodies and get out of this house!" Then begin to praise the Lord because your children are healed. When you do, the disease symptoms will disappear.

If your child is worse the next day, lay hands on him and repeat what you said the day before. If he's worse the day after that, do it again. Keep doing it until the results come. As the days go by, you have to get stronger, not weaker.

The Devil will say, "I ought to wreck the whole family and make them sick, but I can't keep this affliction in here. The head of the house won't let me." When you show the Devil that you don't have any quitting sense, he'll leave.

If you're the head of the house, you need to be strong, especially if your house is full of kids.

In the late 60s, John Osteen was the most popular field evangelist in charismatic circles. He could lift you out of your seat in ten minutes. One

Sunday night when he spoke at our church in Tennessee, the whole church was baptized in the Holy Ghost. Our pastor said, "That's the first time I've ever seen a two-week revival in one day." People were flooding the front of the church. They were talking in tongues all over the room. God's glory had come in and saturated the place!

After a meeting like this, John would call home to find out that one of his children was sick. He would have another tremendous meeting, full of miracles and healings, then call home later to find out that another child was sick. This went on continuously. Sometimes John's wife Dodie would be sick.

He said, "This is crazy! I hold a meeting and God heals people everywhere, then I go to my room and call home only to find that something is wrong with one of the kids. Sometimes I don't even want to call home."

One day he was in their living room about to leave for a meeting when Dodie said to him, "John, you better not go. Some of the children are feeling bad. One is already sick."

He finally got tired of everybody being sick. He said, "Devil, you're not going to make my family sick!" He got all five of his kids together and said, "Come on, kids, we're going to make a choo-choo train." He had them line up behind him — Paul, Lisa, Tamara, Joel and April — each with his hands on the waist of the one in front of him.

Together they marched around the house, yelling, "Devil, you're a liar! You're not going to make this family sick!" Then they marched around confessing, "God has healing power! No devil can make us sick! No devil can set foot on our property! The blood of Jesus keeps us whole!" Like a choo-choo train, they said over and over, "I put the blood! I put the blood! I put the blood!"

You may say, "Brother Norvel, that's silly. I would feel like a nut."

That doesn't matter. Go ahead and do it anyway. If you don't want to, stay sick. Zona thought I was strange; but when I cursed the growths like Jesus told me to, Zona got healed! To keep the Devil away from your family and off your property, you have to pay a price.

God Heals Deformed Girl

I knew a woman who confessed for fourteen years that her deformed daughter was healed. The girl wasn't deformed because of disease; she was born crippled. Her hands and feet were deformed; and her mouth was so twisted she couldn't even eat.

Throughout those fourteen years no one around that woman believed that Jesus would do it, but He did! Jesus made that young girl normal.

Right after the child was born, that mother had started praying, "Jesus, You said in Mark 9:23 that all things are possible to him that believes. You said in Matthew 21:22 that I could have anything when I pray. My daughter is included in all things. I believe for You to come to my house and make my daughter normal."

This woman's family wasn't Full Gospel. They didn't have healing services in their church, but they had a good salvation message. No matter what denomination you are, you have a right to believe the Bible. Sometimes people who have not been baptized in the Holy Ghost can believe the Bible better than a Full Gospel person. All anyone has to do to believe the Bible is to make up his mind to do it. Jesus said in Matthew 21:22, *Whatsoever ye shall ask in prayer, believing, ye shall receive.* God wants you to ask in prayer because He likes for you to be reverent. Then when you believe, this verse says you *shall* — not *might* — receive.

God Isn't on a Time Clock

Your faith will pay off every time. Getting a healing is simple, but you have to talk your faith until the healing manifests. You need to use the right words if you want God to work for you when you are confessing.

This woman used the word *normal.* She talked her faith for fourteen years. Then one day Jesus came to her house and touched the girl in the wheelchair. Ten seconds later, that girl jumped up and ran off, completely normal.

I have told about this mother's faith for years and have appeared with the daughter on television. I teach how your faith can get a total healing for your children until they are grown if they live on your property. I teach that you can't put God on a time clock. For a healing to manifest, it may take years of believing and confessing, or it may take only five minutes. If God delays the manifestation, you won't be glad while you are believing because you want it so badly; but once the manifestation comes, you will see why it was delayed and be glad God delayed it.

Don't try to get your friends to believe with you; that's the worst mistake you can make. Most of them only believe certain things in the Bible and won't confess and believe with you. If that mother had found ten people in a Full Gospel church to believe with her for her daughter's healing, three of them would have dropped off after the first six months. After the first year, she probably would have lost three more. When God hadn't answered in two years, the others would have left, too.

You are dealing with God, not with the people around you. When God says something to you, all He wants you to do is to be intelligent enough to believe it. If you do, then God Himself will come to you.

Confessing the Word of God builds your faith so that you can believe for yourself. Confess the Bible on your own; believe it on your own. If you are the head of the house, you have to believe for yourself. You can go through the house confessing the same as

I can. If God did it for me, He will do it for you. He doesn't love me more than He loves you. When you know your rights in Christ Jesus as head of the house and claim healing for your family, then thank God and praise Him; His power will come into your house and heal.

True Danger of Sin

God will give you an added blessing when you have strong standards for your children. They will be proud of you as I was of my father.

Zona is proud of me. Sometimes she will sit down beside me, lay her head on my shoulder, start crying, and say, "I thank the Lord all the time for giving you to me as my daddy. I can't believe that God would give me a daddy like you. Sometimes I pinch myself to make sure I'm your daughter. If it hadn't been for your faith, I'd be dead now." She was referring to the time I used my faith as head of the house to bring her back after she had backslidden away from God. She had gone so far away from God that she had joined a gang. Five members of her gang — young people — died. I got half beaten down trying to stand in faith to bring her back to God.

When I was in Texas holding a meeting, the Lord manifested Himself to me. He said, "Your faith is strong for healing and strong in other areas, but it isn't strong enough to get your daughter back. She would like to come back to Me, but she can't. The little bit of faith she has left in Me is not strong enough for Me to be able to manifest Myself and come to her. It's not strong enough for her to give up the nightclubs, the new set of friends, and the worldly desires she has been involved in for three years. Those spirits of darkness have grabbed her."

The Lord told me that even though my faith wasn't strong enough to get Zona to come back to Him, it was strong enough to enable Him to manifest Himself to her. He brought her back.

When God repairs something, He makes it better than it was before. Since God brought Zona back out of sin into His family, she loves me now more than she did before. She loves me about three times as much as before because I stood in the gap for her.

In a vision I received years ago, the Lord told me to warn people to stay out of sin. We know that God will forgive us of sin: The price has already been paid for Him to forgive us of sin.

The Lord showed me the real danger of getting into sin. When people get into a certain kind of sin, they like it so well that they can't seem to come back. That often happens to young people as it did to Zona. She almost didn't come back. When this happens, the people want to come back to the family of God, but they can't. The sin gets hold of them too strong. They fall deeply in love with the sensation of whiskey and, as a result, can't ever give up drinking. It takes God's power to give it up. They might be in a place where people can't pray for them, or they might not have any friends who will stand in the gap for them.

Alcoholics don't want to be alcoholics. The world is full of them though, because they got out into sin and couldn't get back. They want to go to heaven, but thousands of them will die alcoholics because they don't want to give up the bottle.

Sometimes your doctrine can become a habit and cause the same problems as an alcoholic's habit. You may have gone to a cold church for years and not want to give it up. Billy Graham says the worst fault that Americans have is that they are creatures of habit. Being a creature of habit can damn your very soul.

Be Flexible

You must break your habits. For eight years I worked with a woman in our town, trying to get her saved. She was single and living in adultery with a married man. About half of her loved God and wanted to get saved, but she just couldn't seem to let go of her sin.

God won't save you just because you want to get saved and go to heaven. You have to lay the sin down. If you are living in sin with another person, you have to give it up if you want Jesus to save you. If you want to get saved because you don't want to go to hell, but you also want to keep your lover, you will have to make up your mind: Do you want Jesus or do you want your lover?

Many people have wanted to get saved before they died, but they went to hell because they didn't want to give up their sin. You have to be willing to give up your sin in order to get saved.

The Gospel will set you free so that you can break your bad habits. Do you have the same meal every morning for breakfast? Do you always eat two eggs well-done, crisp bacon, and light whole wheat toast with a small amount of butter every morning promptly at seven o'clock?

I used to have habits like that, but I don't anymore. I can eat an egg for breakfast, or I can eat vegetable soup! I used to want things a certain way all the time, but now I'm free. I can drink orange juice for breakfast or drink iced tea. It doesn't matter anymore.

When you have to have things the same way all the time, you put yourself in a bad position. When things don't go that way, you easily get upset. Circumstances affect you.

If you are set in your ways, you will have problems in mission work. One time when I was on a mission trip, I had to ride all day long to get to the town. I got to the hotel about thirty minutes before the service was to begin. I was hot and sweaty from the trip and had to climb three flights of stairs to get to my room. After sweating all day, I wanted to take a bath, but the bathtub was dirty. It was about 115% outside and the room had no air conditioner. If I even washed my hair, I would never get it dried. On top of everything else, there were flies in the room. How did I take that? I praised the Lord and prayed in tongues!

Don't let the conditions around you affect your mind so that you start saying, "I'm not going to live under these conditions. This isn't right; I'm the speaker." If a speaker says, "I'm not coming unless I get an air-conditioned room and a king-sized bed," he ought to stay in a little trailer with a cot.

The Filthy Room

When I went to speak at a meeting one time, I stayed with a man who had listened to my tapes. He had fixed a place for me to stay that was terrible. Spider webs were hanging down from the wall over my bed. He helped get my luggage in, then walked off. After seeing those spider webs on top of my bed, I walked into the bathroom. The bathtub was filthy. When I saw that, I started praying in tongues. Then I got the Ajax cleanser and a cloth, got on my knees, and started scrubbing the bathtub. I got a broom and started knocking the spider webs off the bed.

After about two or three days, that man said, "Brother Norvel, your tapes have been a blessing to our family for a long time. I just wanted to see if you lived what you preached. On your tapes you talk as though you can take anything. I wanted to see if you could take this room." Well, I did. I scrubbed the bathtub and wiped off the spider webs.

It's one thing to stand before a group of people and talk. It's another thing to demonstrate what you are talking about. Don't backslide over a dirty bathtub. Keep cool and scrub the dumb thing! It's not hard: just pray in tongues and scrub. You'll even have a sweet spirit about the people when you get through. You can function well in situations like that. I've been through them a number of times.

The Church in Georgia

I went to speak at a Baptist church on a little rock and dirt road way up in the mountains of Georgia. The congregation was made up of corn-fed country people. They would come to church and bring me sauerkraut, pickled beans, and deer meat. Those Baptists started getting baptized in the Holy Ghost and God started healing them. I had been there for one week and the Lord told me to stay for another.

I said, "Lord, I can't. I've got some meetings to preach in Florida."

I was committed to speak at a convention in Florida, so I had planned to close the meeting in Georgia on Friday night. While I was on my knees praying that Friday morning, my plans changed. When you pray, be prepared; anything can happen. After only two or three minutes of praying, God engulfed me and told me to stay there another week.

81

Why did God want me to go up into the mountains of Georgia, out on a little rock and dirt road to a tiny church? He wanted me to go there to cast some devils out of a certain family. I did that and the Lord set that family free. Now they are strong pillars in the church.

The pastor had been working with the family for fourteen years, but he couldn't make progress because he hadn't cast out the devils. The Lord sent me there because He knew I would cast out those devils. When one of the girls who was living in adultery came to church, I broke the power of the devils. I said, "Devils, in Jesus' name, come out of her!" After they came out, the family started getting saved.

I hadn't gone to that little church for financial blessings. The offerings for the week were no more than $150. But during the week as I was at the altar praying, the Holy Ghost came on me and told me to do something the next morning that eventually made me over $100,000. I hadn't been thinking about financial blessings. I had been praying for the people. I asked the Lord, "Why did You bless me like that? I don't need the money."

In answer to my question He said, "I blessed you because you passed My test."

God blessed me because I was flexible and passed His test by obeying the Bible. Because I was flexible and stayed in the mountains of Georgia an extra week when God told me to, God blessed me with over $100,000. Because I was flexible enough to obey God when He told me to confess for Zona's healing, she was healed through my faith as the head of the house.

4

Jesus Heals Through
The Gifts of Healing

Now concerning spiritual gifts, brethren, I would not have you ignorant.

1 Corinthians 12:1

God does not want you to be ignorant of His healing power. It is a gift to the Church. It is only one gift, but it is called *gifts* because the name applies to more than one healing.

There are all kinds of healing gifts to heal all kinds of needs. God has one gift of healing that will lift a person out of a wheelchair. Often when I teach on the gifts of healing, God's healing power will start to come on someone in the congregation. If that person will yield himself to God's power, he will be healed.

Recently I was teaching this message to a congregation of about 1500 people at a Bible school in Florida. I saw a woman in a wheelchair, so I had her pushed down front where she could hear me.

About halfway through my sermon, I looked down and saw the healing power of God all over her. She had been crippled for years; but when that power suddenly came on her, it began to shake her as she sat there. She shook for about five minutes, then stood up!

Another lady who had brought her to the church said the woman had never been able to stand before. God just shook her as she stood there, then she sat back down. As I continued teaching, God would shake her, then she would stand up. She stood up and sat back down five or six times. God must have shaken her for at least thirty minutes. At last, she took a step. Then she took two. The last time I saw her, she was walking out the door of that church! God's power can even get in a wheelchair with you!

Anytime the warm healing power of God begins to come on you, you need to put some action to your faith and yield yourself to it. That healing power is available to you!

God has a gift of healing for cancer patients, another one for flu, another for pain. He doesn't want anyone to be ignorant of His different gifts of healing.

Attend a Word Church

Unless you have a good reason not to, you should go to a church that teaches about the gifts of healing. You ought to belong to a church to have fellowship. If you go to a church that doesn't teach according to the Bible, you can't listen very closely to what you hear.

You may say, "How can I believe in Acts 2:4 that says, *They were all filled with the Holy Ghost, and began to speak with other tongues, as the Spirit gave them utterance,* if the rest of the people in my church don't believe it?"

What the people in your church believe doesn't matter. If you want God to help you, you have to reach the place in your life where what the whole world believes doesn't make any difference. You need to base your believing on chapter and verse in the Bible, not on a church service. God wants you to bypass all men and believe Him. When what you believe is all that matters to you, God will come to you.

As to whether you should stay in a church that doesn't teach according to the Bible, you need to make a choice. Do you have good reasons for staying in such a church?

Sometimes God will send you to a particular church as a missionary. Many churches in America need missionaries. Often when you talk to people in churches, they say, "I've never seen anything like this before."

You need to show them that the only thing that matters is what the Bible says, not the ideas they have grown up believing.

When asked what your reasons are for going to your church, you may say, "Nice people go to my church," or "My family has gone there a long time; my grandfather even built the church building," or "I have so many friends there." These are not good reasons!

You may think your church is a nice place to go, but it might not be such a nice place if it doesn't show you how to get what you need from God. You had better check to see what you need from God and what the people in your church believe. I helped build my church, but that didn't help me believe the Bible.

You might think, "I don't want to change churches." Reason things God's way. Did He tell you to go to that church? I know you love your pastor, but you should listen to him only if he preaches God's Word. You have a right to listen to God's Word.

Unless you have a good reason not to, you should go to the best church in town. It makes no difference what kind of church it is — Methodist, Baptist, or Full Gospel — as long as it teaches according to the Bible. Learn all you can about God. Take your children to a church that isn't ashamed to teach that God will do anything for you.

God set five offices in the church: apostle, prophet, evangelist, pastor, and teacher. (Eph. 4:11.) You should attend a church that allows people who hold these offices to come and share from the pulpit. From time to time a missionary (apostle) should come and encourage the people to never lose the vision of winning lost souls. An evangelist or prophet who has the gifts of the Spirit operating through him should minister to them. Every so often, a pastor from another church should come in and hold a revival. About once a month, a Bible teacher should hold a teaching session. The pastor should demand that the members of his congregation be there, especially those who have sick or lost children.

You can never learn more about what God's Word actually says than from a person who is anointed by God to teach. Every church needs to receive ministry from all five offices.

A cold church is dangerous because God didn't build it. A cold church can damn your soul and your body. You need to go where God boldly heals people. You can't afford to raise your family in a place where God doesn't work. It is easy to get God's healing power working in your body when you have the right teaching.

In order for the gifts of the Spirit to manifest through the pastor, he must have respect for chapter 12 of 1 Corinthians and teach it. If you waste your time in a church that is ashamed to have healing services, sooner or later you are going to suffer. That kind of church is out of God's will. If you fool around with people who know only a little about God, the Devil will come in and you won't be strong enough to throw him out.

All the Gifts Are Important

Some ministers think that the gift of faith means having a great deal of faith, but that's not what it means. The gift of faith gives you supernatural power to do something in the natural that you couldn't do before.

Most churches are so ignorant of the things of the Bible that 50 out of 100 ministers might not be able to name the nine gifts of the Spirit which God has freely given to the Church. They might think that love is a gift of the Spirit. It isn't; it is a fruit of the Spirit. Many ministers wouldn't know that these two are not the same.

Probably 47 out of the remaining 50 wouldn't be able to name and define all nine gifts of the Spirit, then explain how they operate. That leaves about 3. All of the gifts of the Holy Ghost must be in operation in your church, or you won't have very much of a New Testament church.

If tongues and interpretation are operating in a church, many members will think they have all the gifts operating. They have two of them. What about the other seven? All nine gifts are perfect; each is as important as the others. When you have a need, a gift of the Spirit will manifest and help meet that need.

You need to use the gifts to allow them full manifestation.

Years ago when God first gave the gift of healing to Kenneth Hagin, he didn't do much with it. Then Brother Hagin got sick in New York and the Lord said to him, "I brought you before My throne over twenty years ago to put My fingers in the palms of your hands. I have told you over a thousand times to use the gift I gave you then, but you have never done what I wanted you to do with the healing ministry. You kept on teaching and you prayed for the sick occasionally, maybe one night a week. Put your own hands on your own body now, and you will be healed. Then go back to Tulsa and hold a meeting. I'm going to put My healing power in your hands stronger. Even though I put it in your hands years ago, it didn't manifest itself strongly because you never did anything with it."

God desires that all nine gifts of the Spirit come into manifestation in the Church:

> *Wherefore I give you to understand, that no man speaking by the Spirit of God calleth Jesus accursed: and that no man can say that Jesus is the Lord, but by the Holy Ghost.*

> *Now there are diversities* (differences) *of gifts, but the same Spirit. And there are differences of administrations, but the same Lord. And there are diversities of operations, but it is the same God which worketh all in all.*

> *But the manifestation of the Spirit is given to every man to profit withal.*

91

For to one is given by the Spirit the word of wisdom; to another the word of knowledge by the same Spirit; to another faith by the same Spirit; to another the gifts of healing by the same Spirit; to another the working of miracles; to another prophecy; to another discerning of spirits; to another divers kinds of tongues; to another the interpretation of tongues:

But all these worketh that one and the selfsame Spirit, dividing to every man severally as he will.

For as the body is one, and hath many members, and all the members of that one body, being many, are one body: so also is Christ.

1 Corinthians 12:3-12

The manifestation of the Spirit is given to every man. You belong to the Body.

But now hath God set the members every one of them in the body, as it hath pleased him.

And if they were all one member, where were the body?

But now are they many members, yet but one body. And the eye cannot say unto the hand, I have no need of thee: nor again the head to the feet, I have no need of you.

1 Corinthians 12:18-21

The nine gifts of the Spirit are: gift of faith, word of wisdom, discerning of spirits, word of knowledge, working of miracles, gifts of healing, gift of prophecy, gift of tongues, and interpretation of tongues.

You may say, "What good are the gifts of the Spirit? For instance, what good is the word of wisdom?"

The word of wisdom is God speaking in you to let you know what is going to happen in the future.

During the past two years the word of wisdom has come to me three times concerning little children. God told me that in the future He was going to require me to build something for children. I don't know if it will be for 20 children or for 500. The last time God came to me with the word of wisdom, He said, "I am going to visit you in the nighttime by vision. That will be the final time that I will visit you concerning these children. I will show you in detail what to do: how to build the building and where to build it."

I know the building for the children is coming because the word of wisdom is perfect. I'm not perfect; but the gifts of the Spirit are. Through the word of wisdom, God is getting me ready for that project.

Why are the gifts of the Spirit so important? Because not understanding how the gifts operate is dangerous. The gift of faith, the working of miracles, and the gifts of healing are power gifts. Failure to recognize and operate in one gift of the Spirit could cost a person his life.

The gifts of the Spirit can only operate in people's lives as those people allow them to. If your spirit is not in tune with the Holy Ghost or if you are ignorant of the fact that God is trying to show you something, you won't realize the many things that the Holy Spirit is trying to get over to you.

The gifts of the Spirit operate in you for yourself and for others around you.

As The Spirit Wills

The gifts of healing can operate in different ways. When a pastor ministers to the sick, he is obeying the scripture that says, *They shall lay hands on the sick, and they shall recover* (Mark 16:18). But if he and his congregation will believe together that God will work the gifts of healing, it will come as the Spirit wills, quick like the wind.

The gifts of healing is not automatic; it doesn't come every day. In Full Gospel churches, people expect to get ten of their sick relatives healed the first night. Most of the time something like this won't happen.

The Holy Spirit wills to come and heal you if you trust God. Even though you can't tell when the gifts of healing is going to come, once it does, it will absolutely set you free as it did that woman in the wheelchair during the Florida meeting.

When it manifests, the minister doesn't have to pray for anyone. Crossed eyes are straightened, tongues are loosed, and deaf ears are opened. You can't make the gifts of the Spirit operate; they just operate. When all nine gifts began to operate through me several years ago, it just happened.

You may say, "If the gifts only operate as the Spirit wills, how do you get them to manifest in churches where they weren't operating before?"

If you teach about them, claim them, and believe in them, they will come supernaturally. And you must give God freedom.

Give God Freedom

You can't make God do anything. If you try to make Him operate according to the way you have set up your church services, He won't. But if you give Him complete freedom and pray, He will set you free and perform miracles.

One time a crippled girl about fourteen years old was sitting in the back of a church where I was speaking. Suddenly, while I was teaching the Bible, she stood up! The congregation was shocked! In the middle of their uproar over the healing, I had her walk to the front. I asked, "Honey, what happened to you?"

She said, "While I was sitting in the back, my legs began to get warm, then they got hot. I felt strength coming into my crooked, twisted legs! When I made an effort to sit up, I stood up!"

Her teenaged brother had come with her. While he was looking at his sister's knees and legs, he began walking from the back of that large church saying, "This is my crippled sister. I helped her get in here. I helped her get out of the car. I helped carry her in. This is my crippled sister. I helped her get in here!"

He kept repeating this as he stared at her legs.

This was an example of the gifts of healing in operation. God healed that girl on His own as she sat in the back of the congregation. This kind of supernatural manifestation won't happen in a church that doesn't teach, preach, and believe in the gifts of healing.

God Performs Surgery

Because I give the Holy Spirit total freedom in my meetings, He performs great miracles. Occasionally He will say to me, "I want to perform surgery." This happens sometimes once every two years, sometimes once or twice in a year.

When this happens, I can't let anyone play the piano, sing, talk, or move around. If any of this starts, God stops moving. Once everything gets quiet, I call out a certain person and say to the congregation, "Watch the Holy Ghost operate." Usually when I lay hands on this person, he will fall back under the power of the Holy Ghost. Then he just lies on the floor while the Holy Ghost performs surgery on him. Sometimes God's Spirit will operate for two hours.

If something needs to be removed from your body, God will remove it. If you need a part of your body replaced, He will replace it. If you have two missing ribs, He will put them in. I didn't know this kind of power was available for the Church until the first time God performed surgery in one of my meetings.

Let me give you an example of the way the gifts of healing and miracles operate as the Spirit wills.

I knew a little 81-year-old woman who lived close to our church in Cleveland, Tennessee. Because she had solid white hair, everybody called her Sister White. She was a holy, clean-living woman who loved the Lord. Her great faith in God was legendary.

The townspeople tell stories about what God did for her during the many years she served Him. They tell of the time a cyclone destroyed nearly all the houses in town. Everyone except Sister White ran to their basements when they saw the cyclone coming. At times like this, the Spirit of God would come on her. She stood in front of her picture window and said, "The cyclone won't blow my house away. This house belongs to God. I belong to God, and God is bigger than a cyclone!"

The cyclone destroyed the houses on both sides of her, but didn't harm her house.

The Holy Spirit performed surgery on Sister White. She had a big knot on her jaw that had been there for quite a while. One day when she came to church, the knot was gone! There was no scar or sign of surgery on her face. Sister White stood in front of the congregation and said, "The Holy Ghost operated on me this morning!"

As she told her story, the Spirit of God filled the sanctuary. Everybody sat and wept. She said, "This morning I was walking through my house when the Holy Ghost said to me, 'I want to operate on you.' The presence of God suddenly filled the entire house.

"The Holy Ghost said, 'Get a towel from the bathroom, come back to this room, and sit down in the green chair.' When I had done that, He said, 'Spread the towel across your lap,' so I did. Then He said, 'Turn your head sideways.' When I turned my head sideways, the knot on my face suddenly fell off onto the towel!"

Sister White loved God. Because she gave Him freedom to work in her life, the miraculous healing power of God was manifested!

God Removes Diseases

I give the Holy Ghost complete freedom in my meetings. Twice He has told me to speak to diseases and tell them to disappear. After I told diseases to die in Jesus' name, whatever was wrong with any person in the building disappeared.

Church people, including theologians, don't understand what I am talking about when I say, "We obey God; He doesn't obey us." If one of them says,

"Let me tell you how we do it," I say, "I don't want to hear it unless you have chapter and verse to back up what you are saying." I tell them that if they go on, I will hold my hands over my ears. If beliefs aren't based on chapter and verse, they aren't based on truth and they won't work.

Neutral Buildings Allow More Freedom

Many times God will perform more in a neutral building than He will in a church. Why? Because in a neutral building, you are on 50/50 territory with the Devil.

People who hold grudges against others, who don't like their pastor, or who don't like other things about their church, cause a certain spirit to prevail within their church. Unless people spend time loving each other and worshiping God, the Holy Ghost won't have freedom. He won't be able to rule and reign as He should.

Because the Holy Ghost loves you so much, He still blesses whenever He can. But He can't do very much in a church that is so far in the natural realm that it is out of the divine will of God. God will give just a few blessings. When the pastor lays hands on sick people, the Holy Ghost will heal only a few of them.

In an auditorium such as a motel ballroom, God will usually do five times as much as He will in some churches, even Full Gospel churches. I can walk in with my own faith in God's Word and bind the Devil in Jesus' name. God's healing power will flow freely when you let it.

One time in an auditorium meeting, as I was walking to the platform with Charles and Frances Hunter, two cripples got up out of their wheelchairs and walked. That's the way it ought to be!

Because Lester Sumrall and I let God operate freely in a neutral building at a meeting for young people in Chattanooga, Tennessee, God performed many miracles. We cast a devil out of a hippie leader of a Nashville cult. He was on his way to get a load of LSD in Florida to take back and sell to other hippies when his car broke down outside the YMCA ballroom where we were holding our meetings. He walked in the door and up the aisle. He had a beard; hair was hanging down his back; and an Indian headband was stretched around his head. He was wearing a sleeveless shirt, blue jeans, and Indian moccasins. Under each arm he had tied a black bag and was swinging another one. Around his neck was hanging a tooth or some such weird thing.

Brother Sumrall and I had just finished speaking when this hippie walked up and said, "Something is playing tricks on my mind. [I wanted to say, "You're right about that. Something played a trick on you this morning when you got dressed!"] Something told me to come up here."

We told him that "something" was the Holy Ghost. We took his hands and started praying for him. We took authority over that devil in Jesus' name and commanded it to turn him loose. We yelled, "Come out of him!" At that moment as God's power hit him, the hippie broke and began to weep.

God moved strong in that meeting. Brother Sumrall had to go back to South Bend, Indiana, where he pastors a church; but before he left, he said, "Norvel, you ought to keep this meeting going; God is working so freely." I decided to go on for a few more nights.

Two or three nights later several television people came to the meeting. They had been seeing that hippie on different television shows. He said that he had been in the penitentiary three times and that when he came to Chattanooga, he was a bank robber who knew nothing about God. Then he related the story of how he was set free. He said, "When those men cast the Devil out of me, I fell in love with Jesus. I hadn't even known God was real, but I found out that Jesus loves me!"

A man as weird-looking as he was, witnessing about Jesus on television, got the attention of those television people. The Chattanooga paper ran some half-page spreads about him. He was popular around there for a while.

When those television people came to my meeting, one of them said, "We've read in the Bible about casting out devils, but before we heard that hippie, we didn't know anybody did such things today. We've come here to see what's going on."

I said, "God's power isn't a secret. Sit down. I can tell you what's going to happen. [Some of us had prayed for two hours before the service, claiming that God's power would come in and heal the people. We gave God freedom to heal.] We're going to sing a few choruses of praise to God and worship Him for a few minutes. Then two or three young people who have been saved or healed will give their testimonies. After that, one of these young boys will preach; then I'll speak.

"While this is happening, God will come in. One touch from Him will set you free. Jesus can touch cancer and it will leave immediately. The divine healing power of God can flow down from heaven through your mortal body to put every part of it back in shape again. Not only that, it will drive out every symptom of disease and strengthen every bone in your body. His divine healing power will do it. But you have to know that it's available to you. Jesus does good things for you because He loves you.

"Most people believe that Jesus loves them, but they aren't sure what He will do for them. You need to believe Him and turn Him loose in your own spirit. He will do anything you let Him do.

"Get the Word of God inside you. Until you do, you will have your own version of Jesus, and your version won't work. It has to be the same as God's version. You'll find God's version in the Scriptures. You'll find out that He can set you free."

As we were speaking, the glory of God's divine healing power began to come in through the wall to my right. It passed over the congregation and went out through the wall to my left. As it moved slowly over the congregation — a period of about two minutes — people received everything they wanted from God.

One boy whose eyes had been crossed all his life couldn't see anything without thick glasses. When God's divine healing power passed over the congregation, his eyes straightened and he received 20/20 vision. He cried, "I can see without my glasses!" Many people who knew him said that with his eyes straight, he didn't look like the same person.

If you give God's healing power freedom, it will come into manifestation. When it passes over and through people as it did in that meeting, it is so holy, so clean and pure, so powerful that it drives out every disease symptom. That's what God's power is for: to demolish diseases. It gets rid of cancer, blindness, everything!

Because we were in a neutral building talking and preaching about divine healing power, God had freedom to perform all kinds of supernatural acts for people. God should be given the same freedom to move in every church. I am convinced that if people would love each other and worship God more in church, most healing lines would be eliminated. God would have so much freedom, His Holy Presence would so saturate the place, that people would get healed before the healing line ever formed.

To get the gifts operating in your own life, make up your mind that you are a Bible believer, then act like it. The Bible says to seek God for the gifts of the Spirit. (1 Cor. 14:1.) Tell God that you want the gifts!

A Specific Gift of Healing

Occasionally God gives to a minister a certain gift of His healing power. *For to one is given by the Spirit the word of wisdom; to another the word of knowledge by the same Spirit; to another faith by the same Spirit; to another the gifts of healing by the same Spirit* (1 Cor. 12:8,9).

I know of one minister who has a gift of healing for teeth. God fills teeth for nearly everyone he prays for. He has such a strong gift from God that sometimes you can look into a person's mouth and watch as the teeth are being filled.

Another man prays for bad backs, and nearly everybody he prays for gets healed.

God doesn't give these special gifts to everybody. He manifests His healing power in many different ways. After I had worked for God for several years, He put His healing power into my hands as a gift. When I pray, I can feel it coming strong.

Sometimes the gifts of healing will operate along with another gift. The gifts of healing and the gift of the working of miracles are like twin brothers. God often performs a miracle and a healing at the same time.

As we saw before, all nine gifts of the Spirit are perfect. If you believe, you can always count on a gift to manifest when you need it because the gifts are perfect.

Through whatever way you receive God's healing power, once it goes through your body, it will work because it is perfect. God's healing substance comes into your body to combat diseases and to demolish them. When you put your faith to work, that precious power will keep on working until it drives out of you everything that isn't supposed to be there.

5

Jesus Heals Through Anointing With Oil

Is any sick among you? let him call for the elders of the church; and let them pray over him, anointing him with oil in the name of the Lord:

And the prayer of faith shall save the sick, and the Lord shall raise him up; and if he have committed sins, they shall be forgiven him.

James 5:14,15

God is asking the whole human race this question: *Is any sick among you?* (v. 14). God didn't leave you out. He didn't leave out your sick relatives or friends. This verse says *any*. Is *any* sick among you?

Then God gives instructions to the sick person: *Let him* (the sick person, not someone else) *call for the elders of the church* (v. 14).

If someone says, "Brother Norvel, I have a sick friend; but I believe that if you will come and pray,

107

God will heal him," I say, "Let your friend call." You must follow God's instructions exactly.

Verse 14 continues: . . . *let them (the elders) pray over him, anointing him with oil, in the name of the Lord.* Nearly every church believes in praying in the name of the Lord, but some don't believe in using oil. If your church doesn't believe in using oil, go to one that does. This verse can't work for them if they don't have oil. When a scripture says to use oil, it means exactly that: *Use oil!*

Learn The Word

No matter what method God uses to heal you, you must do certain things in order to receive your healing.

Before you can be healed according to James 5:14,15, you first have to be aware that the Word teaches this method of healing. You have to learn what the Bible says.

God's instructions are in the Bible. You don't believe the Bible until you obey it. You can play games with people, but you can't play games with God. God doesn't play games. If you don't have God's Word as the foundation for your believing, if you don't believe the Scriptures and quote them, then you don't have anything. The kind of church building you have or the number of programs you have doesn't matter. God isn't interested in church programs; He is interested in the chapter and verse coming out your mouth.

God will be satisfied with your believing only when you make a certain scripture a part of you just as your right arm is a part of you.

Many people think they believe the Bible, but they don't. Just because you say you do is no sign that you do. You have to show God that you believe the Bible instead of only saying you do. You obey God; He doesn't obey you. You can't go to a Gospel service and expect God to give you everything you want regardless of what you do. God requires certain things of you. He requires you to be willing to do what He wants. To find out what He wants you to do, you must learn His Word — chapter and verse.

You don't have to take a complete course at a Bible school or go to a four-year college to learn how to be healed. God's Word is so powerful that just one verse of Scripture will heal you — if you receive it.

One Verse Away From Healing

You can change things today to get your healing. Even if you are crippled, you can become normal. You are only one verse away from healing.

You can't read the Bible and say, "That's true," then forget about what you have read. You have to begin to quote Scripture. It has to become a part of you. Take the time to study some healing scriptures in the New Testament. Memorize them and get them down inside your spirit.

Every person who has died before his time was only one verse away from complete healing. Most of those people had a Bible lying right by their bed. Many spent thousands of dollars trying to get well. The ones who knew about the Gospel had as many Christians as they could notify to pray for them.

You may say, "I knew a good Christian lady who died. She loved God and had people praying for her." You are trying to argue with God. That lady was one verse away from healing. It's good to pray, but God doesn't promise healing just through prayer.

Your faith is the substance — faith in God's Word. Some people have strong faith, but they don't know what they have faith in. They just have faith. That's not good enough. Just to have faith in Jesus, to have faith that God is God and that He can do anything, isn't good enough either. This general kind of faith has some value, but you have to *show* God that you believe He can do anything.

The way to show God is to prove to Him that you have respect for His Word and that your faith is based on His Word. You must have faith in God's Word. You may believe God and love Him, but that kind of faith isn't good enough if in a time of crisis when you need a manifestation from God, you fail to dig in His Word, find the right scripture, and stand on it without wavering. You must stand boldly, without feelings, claiming the promise as yours because it's in the Bible.

God wants you to have faith in His Word. That is why He says, *Put me in remembrance* (Is. 43:26). God wants you to quote Scripture. He wants you to tell Him what scripture you are believing so that your faith will be based on the Word. That will allow God to perform it and give you what you are asking. Remind God of the chapter and verse you are basing your faith on. It does no good to say, "I don't know whether or not God promises what I'm believing for; I'm just believing." That kind of general praying won't get results. You have to know chapter and verse. To receive the manifestation, you must zero in on God's Word and what he has actually promised.

Find the scripture that covers what you want from God. Boldly take it and stand on it: memorize it and get it into your spirit. Until you do, your mouth won't quote it because the Bible says, *Of the abundance of the heart his mouth speaketh* (Luke 6:45). Scripture goes from your heart to your mouth, then out your mouth to do the work it promised to do. It heals, brings in finances, or does whatever it said it would do.

One girl that I know came from an internationally known family. She was Full Gospel but she died from cancer. She had been prayed for by several thousand Full Gospel, Spirit-filled, tongue-talking Christians. Jesus told me to try to get her to believe one verse of Scripture. I went to her house and said to her, "God told me to come and give you this verse of Scripture so that you could live and not die. If you will believe it, that disease will disappear."

111

When I reached out to pray for her, she broke and began to weep. She wanted to believe, but couldn't. Her mother said, "Brother Hayes, did you know that our daughter has been taught divine healing all her life?"

I wanted to say, "The problem is what you've been teaching her!" Just because the minister of a Full Gospel church prays for the sick and the members believe in divine healing is no sign you will receive healing there. If one thousand New Testament evangelists prayed for you, but you didn't believe the Scriptures, you wouldn't get healed. It makes no difference what other people believe; it's what you believe that counts with God.

When your spirit has been reborn by God, the Greater One comes to live inside you. Luke 17:21 says that the Kingdom of heaven is within you. In other words, the Holy Ghost that lives in your belly (John 7:38) can get you anything that heaven offers you now. The Holy Spirit in you thinks exactly like God thinks. He is a divine Person, Who has come to live in you and give you instructions about heaven. Chapters 21 and 22 of Revelation describe all the good things in heaven.

The Holy Spirit tries to get over to you the things you need; but if you fail to read the Bible, you will be so caught up in the natural realm that you can't listen to Him. He can't get over to you the scripture that you need because it isn't in your spirit. *Faith cometh by hearing, and hearing by the word of God*

112

(Rom. 10:17). When you get the Scriptures inside you, faith will rise up in you for the particular need you have.

When you have a need, memorize one scripture that covers your need. Quote that scripture over and over each day for several days — two or three thousand times, if necessary. When you have done that, the scripture will be inside you. The next time the Devil comes and tries to put something on you, that scripture will begin to come alive inside you. The Holy Spirit will take that scripture into the natural part of you.

The more Word you have learned, the more easily you will be able to fight the Devil. When he comes to you, say, "It is written," and quote the Scriptures.

One day as I was driving down the road, the Spirit of the Lord came upon me and said, "I want you to start teaching My Church to fight the Devil the same way I did." One way He fought the Devil was by casting out devils. The other way is described in the third and fourth chapters of Matthew. After Jesus was baptized by John in the Jordan River, He was driven by the Spirit into the mountains, where He fasted for forty days and forty nights. The Devil manifested and brought temptations to Him. Each time the Devil opened his mouth, Jesus said, "It is written."

If God heals you and the symptoms come back, the Devil will try to talk you out of your healing.

Every time he tries that, just say, "It is written," then quote to him chapter and verse, usually the one verse you are believing. You will whip him every time!

When the Spirit spoke to me that day in the car, He was telling me to read the Bible to the Devil. Satan can't overpower God's Word. He won't give up easily, but he *will* give up, eventually. He gets tired of listening to the Bible, especially when he realizes that you aren't going to give up.

Obey Without Questioning

You have to show God that you trust what He says exactly. If you question or analyze or doubt the Bible, you are not acting as though you trust God. Watch your mouth. One *But, Jesus* . . . will keep the power of God's Word from working for you.

The hardest thing for some Christians to do is read a verse in the Bible, believe it, and then do it. Christians must learn to quit talking and show God some action. When they do, God's power will give them the help or freedom they need.

The disciples couldn't do much of what God wanted because they talked too much. Matthew 14:14-21 describes the miracle of the multiplication of the five loaves and two fishes. Jesus had spoken to a multitude of five thousand men, plus women and children (a total of about 15,000 people), and healed their sick.

The disciples said to Jesus, "We ought to send these people to the villages to buy some food."

Jesus said, "You give them something to eat."

"But, Jesus, we only have two fishes and five loaves of bread." Jesus had said to them, "*You* give them something to eat," not "*I* will give them something to eat." He didn't want to have anything to do with supplying the food. But the disciples started questioning and analyzing. When they started saying, "But, Jesus . . . ," He said, "Bring the loaves and fishes to Me." He looked up to heaven, asked God to bless the food, and prayed, "Thank You, Father, for feeding these people." Then He broke the bread. He had to break all of it Himself; nobody else had enough faith to break it. He gave the food to the disciples, and the disciples passed it out to the people.

Jesus was God manifested in the flesh. If the disciples had obeyed without question, they could have done what Jesus did: They could have broken the bread, passed it out, and fed the entire multitude themselves.

There are several examples, even in the Old Testament, of God honoring the kind of faith it takes to obey without questioning. We are living under a new covenant which puts us in a better position for God to honor this kind of faith and give us what we need. You must learn to obey immediately. If you do, it will change your life.

The Bible is already written and established in heaven. Make up your mind that you can receive great manifestations from God just from one verse. When you do, God's power will give you what that scripture says.

God Performs His Word

When you have learned what the Bible says to do and then have done it, God will perform His Word.

According to Jeremiah 1:12, God Himself looks over His Word twenty-four hours a day with a sharp eagle eye to perform it. He performs His Word — not your version of it. You must do exactly as the Word says.

If you stop quoting a scripture, God stops working. God's Word has already been spoken and written. What it says will automatically be done if you let it. God will perform any verse of Scripture for any person who will obey.

When disease comes and tries to fasten itself on you, those verses from the Bible that you have memorized, those words inside you, have already come out the mouth of God. Those same verses coming out your mouth will bring power and victory.

All you have to do is hunt scripture and stand on it. It will bring you up from a death bed. Again, I state: You are only one verse away from healing. But you have to take hold of the Scriptures and not let go. Any verse of Scripture that promises you something in the New Testament will bring God's power to you. But you have to know that; you have to make that scripture a part of you.

A few years ago, God gave me a new method of teaching to encourage people to obey the Scriptures. He said:

"The invitations for salvation, for the baptism of the Holy Ghost, and any other general invitation are good because the people can receive from Me when they come and ask. But unless I direct you otherwise, I want you to stop giving those invitations at the end of every service. You have been trying to talk people into believing. Instead, have the people do what you teach. If you teach on one subject and then give ten unrelated invitations, the people will have forgotten what you taught them in three days. But if they obey the words you teach, they can take home what they learned.

"If you teach on prayer, have the people pray. If you teach on praying in the Spirit, have them pray in the Spirit. If you teach about the laying on of hands or another means of using faith, have the people come forward and obey what you have taught."

God's help comes when you obey His Word.

Help comes from the Scriptures that you obey yourself. If someone else obeys verses of Scripture for you, those verses will only work in part. God can hardly wait to heal you. All you have to do is obey the Scriptures yourself.

God Will Give You Anything

When you do what God wants, He will do what you want.

The second year I taught at Southern Illinois University, I spoke in big, modern classrooms. The 400 seats were arranged in tiers around the stage. The first night, as I stood looking up into the crowd, I saw a psychiatrist I knew who had brought a large group of people.

As I was teaching that night on the goodness of God, I made a bold statement: "God will do anything for you if you trust Him."

The moment I said that, a woman sitting close to the psychiatrist jumped up and, pointing to her seat, yelled, "It happened right there when you pointed your finger at me!" (I hadn't even known that she was there or that I had pointed my finger at her.)

"What happened?" I asked.

"I had been deaf for thirty years. When you pointed your finger at me, my ears popped open! I can hear everything! My husband and I came to this service with this doctor. We have never been to a service like this before. My husband can tell you that I was deaf. But now I can hear everything! It happened right there in that seat!"

She kept talking like that and wouldn't quit. God made a missionary out of her, and for the next two weeks she worked the town!

The things I am sharing are not hearsay. I was there when God opened that woman's ears. God Who can do anything performs His Word.

If you will obey the Scriptures, God will do anything that the Scriptures say He will do. If you preach a good salvation message — that Jesus loves you so much He died on the cross for you — the Holy Spirit will put the sinners under conviction. They will run to the altar to get saved. They will get saved because you preached good salvation scriptures. If you obey God and preach healing scriptures, God will heal people.

Some people say that salvation is more important than anything God has for you. That kind of thinking will get you mixed up. You need to be saved first. But once you are saved, salvation won't help you if you are dying of cancer. God doesn't have a one-track mind. The Scriptures say that when you get saved, born again by the Spirit of God, God will bring you everything you need for success and victory from the time you get up in the morning until the time you go to bed at night.

When you obey God, He will give you anything. He will make you healthy. He will clear your thinking. He will bring you heaven now.

James 5:14 says to use oil. In order for God to perform His Word, James 5:14,15 must be obeyed exactly.

My mother died at 37 years of age and my oldest brother died at 19 while going to a church that didn't

119

use oil. Our church had a blackboard with a sign over it that said, "Pray for the sick." Under that sign was written my mother's name, "Zona Hayes." We prayed for her, but she died. My brother, Glenn Hayes, put his name there. It stayed there for about a year and a half, then he died.

People all over the country know of someone who died, even though others were praying and praying. They ask me, "Why did he die?" My answer is always the same: "He died because he didn't believe the Scriptures."

I found out that blackboards don't work. God doesn't look over a blackboard to perform it; He looks over His Word to perform it. (Jer. 1:12.) Blackboards aren't scriptural. God looks over elders of the church who are praying in the name of Jesus, anointing the sick with oil, and praying the prayer of faith. God looks over this because it is done according to His instructions in the Bible. Putting a steeple on a building and presenting your version of God won't bring healing. You have to be scriptural.

Don't Depend On Feelings

In one meeting when I had finished teaching on James 5:14,15, I asked the people to line up across the front so I could pray for them. I had been teaching that you must have faith without feelings.

This idea jars the average Christian because people like to have feelings. God gave us feelings, but

120

sometimes we are healed without feeling anything. When my daughter was healed — when those growths disappeared and she suddenly received new skin — there was a quick manifestation from the Lord. Zona didn't feel anything. When you believe for a healing, have faith in God's Word and pay no attention to how you feel. Even if you don't feel it, the power of God is in your body to bring a healing.

I told the people that night, "The beginning of James 5:15 says, *And the prayer of faith shall save the sick . . . .* Save is the opposite of dying. Then it says, *. . . and the Lord shall raise him up. Raise* means getting healed.

"James 5:14,15 will work for anyone who obeys it. Let your faith be in those scriptures because they are being obeyed. If you respect and believe them, your healing will manifest. Put your faith only in God's Word. When I anoint you with oil and pray the prayer of faith over you, you must believe at that moment that you are healed. You must believe even though you may not have any feelings."

I anointed each person with oil and prayed in the name of Jesus. When I reached the end of the line, I went back to the first person and asked, "When I prayed for you, did you feel anything?"

"No."

"How do you know that you are healed?"

"I know because James 5:14,15 says that I am."

As I went down the line, asking everyone the same question, each person answered the same way.

Then one said, "I know I'm healed because the Lord heals."

I said, "You don't understand the principle yet. It won't work for you. What did I teach about tonight?"

"You taught on James 5:14,15."

"When I anointed you with oil and prayed the prayer of faith in Jesus' name, did you feel anything?"

"No."

"How do you know you're healed?"

"I know I'm healed because you taught that James 5:14,15 is the reason I'm healed."

"Now, you've got it." Then I went down the rest of the line. Nobody said he felt anything.

When I finished, the Lord said to me, "Walk up and down in front of the line and teach James 5:14,15 again. They don't have it yet." I had already taught on this for about an hour and a half, but I hammered on for another fifteen minutes. Unless you take a scripture home with you, you don't really have it. I said:

"You are healed because God has already spoken the words in James 5:14,15. His instructions are the truth. You are healed because I have obeyed them in your behalf by anointing you with oil in Jesus' name and praying the prayer of faith for you. You are healed, not because I'm here, but because you have faith in God's words.

"The man who obeys James 5:14,15 in your behalf doesn't have anything to do with your healing. It's the Scriptures that heal you. John 17:17 says the Word of God is true, and John 8:32 says the truth shall make you free. Now, you have to say your faith. The substance is what you say, but you have to put action to your faith. When you leave this building tonight, I want you to walk to your car saying, 'I'm healed because James 5:14,15 has been ministered to me. I'm healed because James 5:14,15 says I am. I'm healed because God's Word has been obeyed in my behalf.'

"If you are married, don't talk much. Save whatever you need to talk about until tomorrow. Have your wife or husband help you quote what I said as you drive home. While you are getting ready for bed, continue to quote it. When you get in bed and say good night, quote it some more. If your mate has to get up early and is trying to go to sleep, then put your head in your pillow as you continue to say it: 'It is written that when the elders of the Church anoint me with oil and pray the prayer of faith, God will raise me up. James 5:14,15 has been obeyed in my behalf; therefore, I am healed. I am healed because the Word says I am.'

"Then say every day, 'My body is healed according to James 5:14,15.' Tell God, 'James 5:14,15 is mine.' Let the Devil know that you accept those scriptures. From time to time, say to the Devil, 'Devil,

James 5:14,15 is true. Jesus is truth, and you are a liar!' "

After the people at the altar had promised to do as I said, I dismissed the service. The next night as I was walking toward the church after parking my car, a businessman called to me. I looked back to see him running toward me. He said, "I've heard James 5:14,15 preached for years, but I never got it until last night. I did what you told us to do. I went to my car quoting what you said; I went home quoting it; I took off my clothes, got in bed, and turned out the lights still quoting it.

"My feet and ankles were deformed. Even though I didn't walk normally, I could at least walk; but I never could run. This church knows how I was. I went to sleep quoting what you said.

"This morning when I woke up I pulled back the covers and put my legs and feet on the floor like I always do. As I was sitting there, I looked down to see that both my feet and ankles were normal! I was healed because of James 5:14,15!"

The Lord decided to come in with the gift of healing. Because the man had faith without feelings, he was healed.

One time when I was invited to speak at a church in New York, the Lord said, "Take a bottle of oil with you." When I finished, I had the people come forward for healing. I gently anointed them with oil in Jesus' name, and the Lord healed them. Catholic

nuns came up and received their healing. So many
people came up that I had to bring them on the stage.

God moved so strongly, healing so many, that
finally there wasn't room left, even on the stage.
Sometimes when a person in a healing line gets the
manifestation right then, his body can't stand it, and
he falls under God's power. I had to wait until some
of the people were able to get up off the floor to make
room for more.

After the service, the pastor said, "Mr. Hayes,
my wife and I have been praying for several years
for God to send His power into this church."

God sent me with a bottle of oil and James
5:14,15. I didn't need anything else! Because we
learned God's Word and obeyed it, God performed
His Word and healed the people.

6

Jesus Heals Through
Special Miracles

*And God wrought special miracles by the
hands of Paul:*

*So that from his body were brought unto the
sick handkerchiefs or aprons, and the diseases
departed from them, and the evil spirits went
out of them.*

Acts 19:11,12

Healing For Those Far Away

Acts 19:11,12 is the best passage to use when
praying for friends and relatives who don't live
near you.

Several years ago while I was speaking at a Full
Gospel Business Men's Convention in Hamilton,
Ontario, a lady from Buffalo, New York, brought a
handkerchief for me to pray over. It seems that her
daughter-in-law, who had intended to come to the
convention, was put in the hospital a few days before

the meeting. I prayed over the handkerchief and told the lady to have her daughter-in-law put in on the afflicted place. By the time she reached the hospital, her daughter-in-law had already undergone a complete hysterectomy (removal of ovaries, fallopian tubes, and womb). Also her intestines had been removed and placed at the sides of her body. She eliminated body wastes in a bag hanging at her side.

The woman placed the handkerchief on her daughter-in-law, and God healed her. Today she has received new organs!

When God creates new wombs, ovaries, and tubes, that is a special miracle. If you went to the average church and asked the average Christian, "Do you believe that Jesus makes new wombs through handkerchiefs?" he would say, "We don't want to get our good solid church off on something so far out."

The Bible teaches that God will perform special miracles through a handkerchief or cloth laid on a sick person's body. The diseases will depart; the demons will be driven out.

God will do special miracles to give you anything you need if you will obey His instructions in the 19th chapter of Acts.

God Wants To Use You

God wrought special miracles by the hands of Paul. God can't use Paul's hands today. God wants to do miracles through your hands.

128

You may say, "God has never performed miracles through my hands." But He wants to! He wants to heal and bless people through you.

You can know God, be healed by Him, and have His gifts operating through you just as well as anyone. You don't have to be a famous evangelist. Sister White, that little 81-year-old lady who lived by herself in a tiny house, probably knew God better than anybody I have ever met. She knew God so well because she obeyed Him. She knew God in a completely different realm than most people do. God talked to her.

I have taken internationally known evangelists and preachers to her house. When she started talking, they got blessed.

One preacher I know, who had just returned from preaching around the world, stopped in Cleveland, Tennessee, to see me. When I asked if he would like to get blessed, he said, "Sure."

"Then I'll take you to meet somebody who knows God better than you do. Get in the car."

When I pulled up in front of Sister White's tiny house, the evangelist said, "Norvel, what are you doing?"

I said, "The person who lives in this house knows God better than you. Don't judge; just be nice. You are going to be blessed."

When we walked into the house, Sister White said, "Brother Norvel, where have you been? I've been waiting to see you for so long. Why didn't you come to see me? It's so good to have you." (Whenever she saw me, she said the same thing.)

"Sister White, I've had things to do, but I brought a friend who has been preaching around the world. I wanted him to meet you and get blessed. Tell him about the Holy Ghost operating on you, Sister White."

So she began her story: "Oh, yes. I had a knot on my jaw that had been there for quite a long time . . ."

Each time she told about what had happened, the glory of the Lord came on her. I looked over at the preacher. That evangelist, who had just come back from preaching around the world, was weeping.

I said to him, "Get on your knees and let Sister White bless you." Sobbing, he dropped to his knees, ready to be blessed.

"Sister White, I want you to put your hands on my friend and ask Jesus to bless him." By that time she hardly knew where she was.

She put her hands on him and just said, "Glory, Jesus. Bless, Jesus; oh, Jesus, bless."

God's glory was rolling in that little white house. He gave that evangelist a bath in the Holy Ghost. He used a little elderly lady to bless a famous evangelist. You don't have to be famous for God to use you.

Anything I do, you can do too, if you are born again. If I can believe a certain scripture, you can believe it. If I can cast the Devil out of someone, you can. If I can lay my hands on sick people, allowing God's power to heal them, you can. God can heal through your hands too! There is nothing supernatural about me. You can do anything I can do; maybe you could do things better.

It's not what you *can* do, but what you *do* that makes the difference. When you do what God's Word says, the blessings of God come on you. Many people know how to do things better than I do; but if I make a stumbling effort, God will give me the blessings. A particular theologian, who knows he is smarter than I am, can't understand why God doesn't bless him the way He blesses me.

You must seek God for different things. You have to put Him first. The Bible promises that if you put the Gospel first, all other things will be added unto you. (Matt. 6:33.)

Put God First

God will manifest Himself when you put Him first, when you talk about Him and sing about Him. When you say He will do something, He does it. Not only will He manifest Himself in different ways, He will manifest Himself by giving you anything you want.

You don't meet very many people who have received manifestations from heaven like I have. The Lord blessed me with over $100,000 after I stayed another week at that little Baptist church in Georgia. I received over a quarter of a million dollars after I was obedient to pass out tracts in Fort Lauderdale, Florida. I put the Gospel first in both situations.

Most ministers of the Gospel, those who are walking in the calling of the Lord, won't go to Fort Lauderdale and pass out tracts for a week, especially if they have a public ministry. They won't go to a little church on a dirty road back in the hills where they get deer meat as offerings from the mountain people.

Don't worry about expenses or anything else; just go where God tells you to go.

For as many as are led by the Spirit of God, they are the sons of God (Rom. 8:14). Once you have made up your mind to obey the Holy Ghost, you will see great manifestations of healings and workings of miracles. After the people are blessed, God will bless you. Third John 2 says, *Beloved, I wish above all things that thou mayest prosper and be in health, even as thy soul prospereth.* If you make up your mind to obey the Holy Ghost, He will give you blessings as great as the quarter-million-dollar blessing He gave me.

Put the Gospel first and all other things shall be added unto you.

Follow the Leading of the Holy Spirit

When I was in Alabama, the Lord showed me that you have to learn how to be led by the Spirit of God when you are out ministering because the Spirit of God leads people in different ways. You can't just minister one day unless God told you to.

When I teach on having faith without depending on feelings, people are usually healed without having any feelings. In one service, God may cause people to drop to the floor and weep before the healing power begins to come upon them.

When I teach the Bible, I follow the leading of the Holy Spirit. God told me once, "I want you to teach the people what I have taught you. I want you to teach My Word." You teach what God has taught you. The Lord requires me to teach on healing. But I don't have to think about what I'm going to say. I never have to hunt for words because God touches me divinely and puts words inside me. I could stand before a group and teach on healing for two months because the Holy Ghost will teach through me.

When God first started teaching through me that way, I would shake my head later and say, "Was that me? I can't believe I said all those things."

If God Can Trust You, He Will Promote You

The more that God can trust you, the more He will bless you and promote you. *He that is faithful in that which is least is faithful also in much: and he that is unjust in the least is unjust also in much* (Luke 16:10).

He will trust you first with the Gospel. Then He will trust you with some small thing besides the Gospel to see how you do. If you do a good job with that, He will trust you with something else.

If you show God that He can trust you, He will bless you more than you could have ever dreamed possible. The blessings will come to you at the most unique and unexpected times. You won't even be thinking about them and they will come to you. God blessed me that way by healing Zona's warts. Always put the Gospel first; then all other things will be added unto you. When you diligently seek God and let the Devil know that you mean business by confessing who you are in Christ Jesus, God will reward you and give you your healing.

Let God Use Your Hands

When you put God first, He will heal through you. Look at your hands and think, *God will bring miracles, special miracles, to people through my hands.*

Let Him use your hands. When I lay my hands on handkerchiefs or cloths to be taken to the sick, I pray like this:

"Father, in Jesus' name, I lay my hands on these cloths and claim that Your healing, miracle-working, and delivering power goes into them to drive out evil spirits and demons. As these cloths are put on sick bodies, all the diseases will disappear from those bodies. All evil spirits will go out of the bodies completely, in Jesus' name, and leave the people every whit whole.

"If there are bodies that need special miracles, the Spirit of God shall perform them. Father, in Jesus' name, I claim that the power of God goes into these cloths and handkerchiefs to do the work that God intended and promised that they would do in Acts 19:11,12. It is done, in Jesus' name."

7

Jesus Heals Through
Praying For Others

*Confess your faults one to another, and
pray one for another, that ye may be healed. The
effectual fervent prayer of a righteous man
availeth much.*

James 5:16

The Word of God says you should pray for
others because when you do, you will be healed.

This is an area of healing I had never taught
until just recently. As I was on an airliner, flying to
Honolulu, the Lord began to speak to my heart about
healing. He said, "I want you to teach the people in
Honolulu on a subject you have never taught
before." Then He showed me James 5:16. He said, "If
you will have the people in your meetings who need
healing to pray for another person, then they will
receive their healing as they do."

When I got to Honolulu, I was scheduled to
speak in a church service on Sunday night, so I spoke

on healing. Then I taught this scripture from James. I told about the importance of praying for one another that you may be healed, as James 5:16 says.

When I had finished teaching, I said:

"Now, this is my first public invitation based on James 5:16; but God told me that He would heal people according to that verse just the same as He heals on any other verse in His Word that promises healing. So let's just take God at His Word. The Bible says God can't lie, so we can get healed through James 5:16: *Pray one for another, that ye may be healed.*"

There were several hundred people in the church that night. When I gave the invitation for people to come forward for healing, a bunch of people came up.

When everybody got down to the front, I said, "Now, I want each of you to turn to another person right now and begin to pray for them. Pray that they be healed. Don't pray for yourself. This scripture in James doesn't say anything about praying for yourself. It says pray for one another. So you start praying for the person next to you, and God will heal you too!"

As those people were praying, the Lord began to heal them all over the place! Then a strange thing began to happen: As they were praying for another person's healing, God found so much favor in it that He began to baptize them in the Holy Ghost. One seventeen-year-old boy who had just gotten saved was praying for another person. As he prayed, a language began to bubble up out of him. Before he knew what had happened, he was baptized in the Holy Ghost and speaking in tongues!

The Holy Spirit really worked that night and brought blessing to the people. It was a beautiful experience. That was my first time to give an invitation based on James 5:16, but it won't be my last!

Pray one for another, that ye may be healed.

Prayer For Healing

We don't have to pay for healing: It's a free gift to the Church. To get your healing, you have to make up your mind that it is for you, then ask for it, and take it. You have to pass God's test over chapter and verse by watching yourself and making sure the words you speak agree with God's words. If you put the Gospel first and confess what you want, God will give it to you. You can enjoy heaven on earth now.

To get God's healing power to work, no matter what the method, keep everything simple and give God freedom. Simple faith pleases God. Be still. Know that God is God. Know that the Bible is exactly what John 17:17 says it is: the truth. According to John 8:32, the truth will set you free! God's Word is truth and it will set you free!

Stop wondering whether or not the Lord will heal you. The Devil and human beings try to put that thought in your mind. Don't express that thought through your vocabulary; get it out of your mind and out of your system!

If Jesus has ever healed one person, He will heal you. God's healing power is *always* available. Jesus will heal you every time!

If you need healing, pray this prayer from your heart:

I thank You, Jesus, because my name is written in heaven. I have a right to God's healing power. I confess with my mouth because I believe in my heart that the healing power of God Almighty is raging through my body to bring a cure to me. God's power is in my body now, working to give me a miracle of healing.

Thank You, Lord, because I'm healed. I'm not going to be healed; I'm healed now, in Jesus' name!

Conclusion

Every person in the world needs to know about God's healing power. They need to know the ways they can receive healing.

Our hospitals are packed with sick people who need the healing power of God. There are some churches with people who know how to pray for the sick, but there are few places where the people can learn how to receive their healing. It's a terrible thing to be sick and not know how to get healed. People want to be healed, but they don't know how to receive it.

It's the simplest thing in the world to get healed: just obey the Scriptures and show God respect for His Word.

He sent his word, and healed them.
Psalm 107:20

Books by Norvel Hayes

Endued With Power

How To Live and Not Die

*The Winds of God
Bring Revival*

*God's Power Through
the Laying on of Hands*

The Blessing of Obedience

*Stand in the Gap
for Your Children*

*How To Get
Your Prayers Answered*

*Number One Way
To Fight the Devil*

*Why You Should
Speak in Tongues*

Prostitute Faith

What To Do for Healing

*How To Triumph
Over Sickness*

*Financial Dominion —
How To Take Charge
of Your Finances*

The Healing Handbook

*Rescuing Souls
From Hell —
Handbook for
Effective Soulwinning*

How To Cast Out Devils

Radical Christianity

*Secrets to Keeping
Your Faith Strong*

*Putting Your Angels
To Work*

Know Your Enemy

**Available from your local bookstore,
or by writing:**

Harrison House
P.O. Box 35035 • Tulsa, OK 74153

Norvel Hayes shares God's Word boldly and simply, with an enthusiasm that captures the heart of the hearer. He has learned through personal experience that God's Word can be effective in every area of life and that it will work for anyone who will believe it and apply it.

Norvel owns several businesses which function successfully despite the fact that he spends over half his time away from the office, ministering the Gospel throughout the country. His obedience to God and his willingness to share his faith have taken him to a variety of places. He ministers in churches, seminars, conventions, colleges, prisons — anywhere the Spirit of God leads.

For a complete list of tapes and books
by Norvel Hayes, write:
Norvel Hayes
P. O. Box 1379
Cleveland, TN 37311
*Feel free to include your prayer requests and comments
when you write.*